The French Influence

The French Influence on English Education

by W. H. G. Armytage

Professor of Education
University of Sheffield

LONDON

ROUTLEDGE & KEGAN PAUL

NEW YORK: HUMANITIES PRESS

*to Bill Lyons, for twenty one
years friendship*

*First published 1968
by Routledge & Kegan Paul Ltd
Broadway House, 68–74 Carter Lane
London, E.C.4*

*Printed in Great Britain
by Willmer Brothers Limited
Birkenhead, Cheshire*

*SBN 7100 4222 1(C)
SBN 7100 4216 7(P)*

THE STUDENTS LIBRARY OF EDUCATION has been designed to meet the needs of students of Education at Colleges of Education and at University Institutes and Departments. It will also be valuable for practising teachers and educationists. The series takes full account of the latest developments in teacher-training and of new methods and approaches in education. Separate volumes will provide authoritative and up-to-date accounts of the topics within the major fields of sociology, philosophy and history of education, educational psychology, and method. Care has been taken that specialist topics are treated lucidly and usefully for the non-specialist reader. Altogether, the Students' Library of Education will provide a comprehensive introduction and guide to anyone concerned with the study of education, and with educational theory and practice.

J. W. TIBBLE

One of the most characteristic features in English history, it seems safe to say, is insularity. Here, as in an earlier booklet on the influence of American education, Professor Armytage throws down barriers and opens up many avenues of enquiry. It may be hoped that students will follow up some of these, with the help of the comprehensive bibliography, for comparative historical study has much to offer. They can hardly fail to enjoy a book which the author has so clearly enjoyed writing.

B. SIMON

Contents

Foreword

'What I gained by being in France was learning to be better satisfied with my own country.' Such quintessential English prejudice could only come from Dr. Johnson. Yet he was forced to admit that 'the French have a book on every subject'. Even the Francophile Thomas Jefferson was afflicted with the same dual vision of France. 'Never was there a country where the practice of governing too much had taken deeper root and done more mischief' he wrote at one time, whilst at another he maintained that, next to his own, France would be the country he and the 'travelled inhabitants of any nation' would choose to live.

Since that time travel, both enforced and voluntary, has increased enormously and Englishmen have found less and less cause to be satisfied with their own country's insular additions to dukes, duodecimalism and dullness. Indeed by 1960 it was being said 'Great Britain is declining in an orderly fashion while France advances in confusion' (Aron, 1960, 4). Certainly after 1960 *Le Plan* 'suddenly became one of the most frequently encountered topics in business circles' wrote a professor of economics at Yale, and a visit to the Commissariat du Plan became 'almost an essential status symbol in upper business, government, and academic echelons' (Chamberlain, 1965, 2).

This book aims to provide a map for students of French and/or education in colleges and universities to see the relationships of these two countries from the standpoint of the title. It in no way prevents, indeed it is to be hoped that it will stimulate, the reader to think of the influence of England on France over the same period.

As we move towards closer association an appraisal of French practices and institutions which have affected the English, from the very solid persons of the eleventh-century Normans to the seventeenth-century Huguenots, from the eighteenth-century Catholic émigrés to the twentieth-century engineers on Concorde, is called for. What should have been an extremely sophisticated cross cultural traffic-plan has, for sheer reasons of space, to become a simple road map. But for those who want to plot more detailed flow diagrams, a bibliography is provided. Like Chinese boxes, some of the books in this contain bibliographies in themselves.

W.H.G.A.

'They order' said I 'this matter better in France'

LAURENCE STERNE, *A Sentimental Journey* (1768)

1

The not uncommon tongue

Gallicisms

'England is for the French something of a museum of
national antiquities.' So John Orr (1948, 26), saw the
end result of 'the constant interchange, borrowing, and
re-borrowing of ideas that has gone on for close on nine
centuries between the two countries'. To him, this 'has
inevitably created similarities of mind-processes, of
methods of thought and presentation of ideas' that link
the two countries together in close spiritual affinity.

Especially is this true of the English language. 'There
are thousands of words and phrases' wrote H. W. Fowler
(1937, 210), 'that were once Gallicisms, but, having
prospered, are no longer recognisable as such.' They
prospered when aired; the airing producing, over successive generations, words like *annexe, bureau, café,
dèpôt, élite, faux pas, gauche, habitué, idée fixe,
jeu d'esprit, laissez faire, métier, naïve, outré, pique,
qui vive, rapport, sang-froid, tour de force* and *verve.*
These, like *mayonnaise* and *gourmets,* have been used
with *panache* as if they were of English origin. So, too,
expressions like always, behind-hand, to burst out cry-
ing, to drink to, to flatly refuse, fool's mate, to go for,
to hot-foot, to make bold, to sit still, take heart, are

some of the many native Anglo-Saxon words that are used with a French turn of phrase.

Such linguistic influence made itself apparent by the end of the tenth century. The missionary spirit of the French Cluniac Order, plus the Norman education of Edward, son of Ethelred the Unready, meant that by 1042 the spiritual and temporal officers of the court were French. So that when William the Conqueror arrived, their speech was not quite as alien as might have been expected.

Angevin variants

Just as the Norman conquerors spoke the French of Normandy and Picardy, so their Angevin successors brought in the language of central France. The first used *k* where the second used *ch*; the first used *ch* where the second used *s*; the first used *w* where the second used *g*; the first used *g* where the second used *j*. Thus we acquired both *catch* and *chase*; *launch* and *lance* and *warden* and *guardian* and *gaol* as well as *jail*. In this way the same French word came in two different forms and often with different meanings (Bradley, 1904, 87).

The linguistic heritage of so long a period of French rule also extended the use of Latin. This can be seen in the concealed images embodied in everyday articles in the classroom, like the easel which comes from *asellus* (=a little ass) and emerges in its true image as the modern 'clothes-horse'. That traditionally forgetful craftsman, the plumber, derives his name from *plumbum* (=lead), whilst the carpenter was originally *artifex carpentarius* (=maker of wagons). A happy hunting ground for those who care to pursue these further is afforded by the Oxford English Dictionary.

Its chief result was that the language of politics and the law is French. *Act, assize, bill, council, court, jury, judge, justice, manor, mayor, prison, Parliament,* and *royal* no less than *tax* are superimposed on institutions they modified or described. So are the ranks of our landed gentry—*duke, marquis, viscount, baron*—over the traditional Anglo-Saxon *cnicht.* Being warlike, the Normans gave us *armour, battle, banner, fortress, siege* and *standard*; commercial, they gave us *butcher, barber, chandler, cutler, draper, grocer, mason* and *tailor.* And with these a host of surnames, place-names, and even relationships—*aunt, cousin, niece, nephew* and *uncle.*

Administrative words like *rent, treasure, accord, justice, peace* and *privilege*; religious terms like *charity, miracle, nativity* and *procession*; military words like *standard, ensign, banner, pennant*; clothing terms like *sandal* and *mantle*; household terms like *basin, furnace* and *lamp* all show how they penetrated.

The University of Paris

The initial substitution of Norman for English schoolmasters (Leach, 1915, 103) was followed by the almost complete interchangeability of church officers. Indeed just a century after the Conquest, an Englishman, John of Salisbury, became Bishop of Chartres just as Pierre des Roches became Bishop of Winchester. French schools at Chartres, Laon and Angers were followed by a University at Paris for which an Englishman, Joscius of London endowed the first college in 1180.

When Henry II wanted to stop students going to Paris after the murder of Beckett, he offered them a haven at Oxford, near his royal palace at Woodstock, where the first English university took root on Parisian lines. Later, after a migration to Cambridge, a college, Pembroke, was founded there by a Frenchwoman, Mary de Valence. This college, like others at Oxford (Exeter and Queen's) encouraged the speaking of French.

By 1360 mutual interchange between the two countries was such that by the end of that year subjects of both England and France were to be free to enjoy mutually the privileges of the universities of the two countries

3

'comme il povoient faire avant ces presentes guerres et commes ils font a present'. Indeed so widespread was the use of French by the beginning of the fourteenth century that P. Meyer considered it had a good chance of becoming the national language of England (Lambley, 1920, 8).

The results of the Hundred Years War

The Treaty of Bretigny also marks the high watermark of English hegemony in Western France. A hundred and fifty years before, in 1214, only La Rochelle and Aquitaine had remained of the enormous holdings in France built up since the Norman Conquest by English Kings (Normandy, Touraine, Anjou, and Poitou). In 1259 the King of England gave a virtual promise not to try and recover them. Moreover he was only allowed to keep part of Aquitaine if he paid homage for it. Yet by 1340 the English King had assumed the title of King of France and twenty years later, by the Treaty of Bretigny, had obtained the whole of Western France, including the river mouths (Guyenne, Poitou, Saintonge, Angoumois, Rouergue, and part of the Pas de Calais) only to be driven out of it all again, except Calais and Guyenne, within another twenty years. By another swing of the see-saw in 1436 the English were occupying Paris and virtually held half of France, yet by 1453 they were once more confined to the foothold of Calais. This vestige they lost in turn a century later.

The Hundred Years War flexed the emergent technologies of the two countries, especially when Flemish weavers, taking fright after the battle of Roosebecke (1382), emigrated to England: the first of a long series of such migrations.

Cannon gave the French further victories at Formigny (1450) and Castillon (1453) enabling them to expel the English from France, leaving Calais as a vestigial appendix to a once great empire.

War also incubated nationalism in the schools. Whereas

in 1327, ten years before it broke out, children in schools were construing their lessons in French 'as so they heveth seth the Normans came first into England', by 1377 English had replaced French in the schools (Legouis and Cazamian, 1928, 102). It had already (1362) been declared the language of the law courts.

During this long war, new French influences crept in. Geoffrey Chaucer, the London vintner's son, when taken prisoner whilst on active service and then ransomed, found himself more interested in French poetry than in his proper business, politics. He adopted the octosyllabic couplet, dropping it later in favour of the Italianate heroic couplet. Thus he wrote, of one of his Canterbury pilgrims, that

> Frensch she spak ful faere and fetisly,
> After the scole of Stratford atte Bowe,
> For Frensch of Paris was to hir unknowe (Prologue I, 122)

Chaucer was so basically French in outlook that a French critic remarked: 'when Chaucer forsakes France, he is a little denaturalised' (Legouis, 1928, 138).

The invention of printing

Even when the greatest technological innovator in British education began his work in 1474, he had to place French words beside English ones to make himself understood. Having spent the best years of his life in Flanders, William Caxton encountered the printing press at Bruges, and was so well instructed by Colar Mansion the printer that he was able to publish a translation of a French book.

Not only was the first English printed book a translation from the French, it was also published in Bruges. So was the second. Caxton returned to England and set up a press near Westminster Abbey where he translated French stories of chivalry, Chaucer's works of poetry and the *Aeneid*. Inspired, on his own admission, by 'the

5

fair language of French, which was in prose so well and compendiously set and written', he wanted to make French medieval romances more available. Even his most patriotic author, Sir Thomas Malory, had to pretend that he had translated his *Morte d'Arthur* from a French book.

Though French was replaced as the language of educated men it was kept alive by Latin. English was a weak instrument employed by writers 'in a manner so meanly, bothe for the matter and handelynge, that no man can do worse'. So the schoolmaster Roger Ascham in the preface to his *Toxophilus* (1545) saw his countrymen's use of their own language.

In print as on the high seas the English writer was as ethical as Francis Drake, prompting Sir Sidney Lee to say that 'future historians of literature are bound ... to face the ethical problems which exist when the author presents his readers with a translation from a foreign tongue without any warning that his work is the offspring of another brain!' For even so-called English translations from the Greek and Latin are versions of French ones. As Sir Sidney continues

> The number of avowed Elizabethan translations from the French is legion. At the end of the sixteenth century there was no French treatise of any genuine interest on science and medicine, or on any of the practical arts of life, such as gunnery, gardening, or needlework, which was not quickly clothed in an English dress.

and concludes 'the debt that Elizabethan culture owed to French culture is not easily overestimated'. (Lee, 1906, 86).

But the sophistication of the native language was in hand. Sir Thomas Wilson's *Arte of Rhetorique* (1553) denounced 'inkehorn terms', 'outlandish English', Anglo-Norman legal language and Chaucerian archaisms. The severing of yet further links with the continent, through the dissolution of the monasteries and the outbreak of the religious wars made the rift with France complete. As if to symbolise this, the last remaining British possession in France, the port of Calais, was lost as well. With the variant hostile postures to France were to be adopted for two and a half centuries, the English language flexed its muscles.

The endless borrowing: 'franglais'

Yet the borrowing of French words by no means ceased. Military and naval terms like *pioneer, pilot, sally, colonel, volley, cartridge, rendezvous, portmanteau* came in together with others used in eating, like *fricassée,* or on the stage like *scene, grotesque* and *hautboy.* Indeed a 'widespread fashion for introducing French words and phrases into ordinary conversation' grew up that prevailed after the Restoration (Serjeantson, 1961, 161). Recently, after compiling a most exhaustive list of such introductions, she concluded that 'the nineteenth century introduced more French words into this country than any period since Middle English' (Serjeantson, 1961, 165).

In another connection, it has been pointed out that the number of French words and phrases in current use in England has increased from 16 per cent in the Middle Ages to 46·9 per cent in our own day (Bliss, 1966, 28). In other words nearly half the total number of foreign words and phrases in current English are French. Just over a quarter are from the classical languages and less than a quarter from the remaining modern languages. So there is some justification for M. Etiemble's concept of '*franglais*', and for the Red Queen to say in *Through the Looking Glass* (1871): 'Speak it in French when you can't think of the English for a thing'.

2
Huguenots

England as asylum

As an asylum, England was invaded by waves of refugees
from the continent. These waves were set in motion by
the establishment of the Inquisition in Italy (1542) or
by the cruelty of the Duke of Alba in the Low
Countries, or by the Catholic zeal of the Kings of France.
To keep track of these immigrants a frequent census
of aliens was taken and all of them were, after 1552,
obliged to attend either their own or the English
parish church. Foreign churches were obliged to send the
Archbishop of Canterbury a list of their communicants,
and these were entitled to apply for letters of denization
enabling them to practice a craft or trade. From these,
and from the census of aliens, names of French teachers
can be and have been recovered.

Such letters of denization were taken out in 1566 by
Claude de Sainliens, a Huguenot who anglicised his name
to Holyband. He has left us a picture in his *French
Littleton* (1566) of the school he kept in St. Paul's church-
yard, where his method, as outlined in *French Schoole-
maister wherein is most plainlie shewed the true and
most perfect way of pronouncinge of the French Tongue*

(1573) was practised. His publisher was another Huguenot, Thomas Vautrollier, whose widow married Shakespeare's friend, fellow Stratfordian and printer, Richard Field. A better known Huguenot was to be immortalised by Shakespeare as the French herald in *Henry V*. For Christopher Montjoy was Shakespeare's landlord in Silver Street, Cripplegate, where he was kept by the proceeds of his hairdressing business.

The name and its significance

These French Protestants took their name from the German term for confederates, *Eidgenossen*. There are others who say it comes from the name given to the protestants of Tours who used to assemble by night near the gate of King Hugo and howl like banshees. Yet further, less kindly, explanations are advanced, like *Hussgenossen* (disciples of Huss), *Duganel* (owlish howlers of psalms) or *Aignos* (deformed). Indeed one derivative (Tolln, 1901, 327) is from the term pot or pan, implying contempt. Certainly non-Huguenots had reason to fear them for they worked hard, possibly because they were virtually excluded from official life, but probably because their schools of learning, no less than their association in consistories and synods, fostered the spirit of self-help. They worked 310 days in the year to the Catholics 260 (Lane Poole, 1880, 9). Such industrious habits commended themselves to the preachers. 'I wish' said one, 'we could collect together such valuable persons in this kingdom, as it would be the means of ensuring the kingdom's prosperity.' His words looked like coming true. Paper making, muslin, hop gardens and fruit farming effected such transformation that it was said that

Hops, reformation, bayes and beer
Came to England all in one year.

Huguenot interest in science

Huguenot interest in scientific education was admired as early as the sixteenth century. The importance of the lectureship in mathematics established by the great Huguenot Peter Ramus (who was murdered by 'the blockish Sorbonnists' in 1572) in Paris so impressed the chaplain of the English Embassy in Paris that he urged his countrymen to do likewise. The chaplain's passionate concern was to enable Englishmen to compete more efficiently with the French and Spanish in the colonisation of America. The chaplain, Richard Hakluyt, began his career as a literary propagandist for such colonisation by publishing in 1582 an account of the attempted colonisation of Florida made twenty years earlier by the Huguenot leader Jean Ribaut.

After the massacre of St. Bartholomew's day in 1572 and the triumph of the Catholic League in 1585 Huguenots flocked in such numbers to England that they numbered nearly 10,000 by the end of the sixteenth century. Given a church of their own, in Threadneedle Street, with others in various provincial towns, they presented such a thriving picture that Sir Sidney Lee remarks:

> Many mechanical arts were greatly improved by these humble *émigrés*. Their pastors often showed scholarly attainments, and their medical practitioners gave proof of unusual skill ... They tended to raise the standard of intellectual efficiency and of material comfort in their English environment (Lee, 1910, 302).

The Huguenots were no less active in France, founding a university at Saumur and an academy at Die in 1604. With Sedan and Montauban these were accorded by English universities 'a rank equal to their own' (Agnew, 1871, i, 17). In these and other Protestant schools the harsh rigours of the doctrine of predestination were mitigated by the view that 'grace' was more universal than had hitherto been supposed. Sedan was especially a centre for the reconciliation of Protestant ideas thanks to the efforts of Phillipe de Mornay, nicknamed 'The Huguenot Pope'.

The University of Montpellier

But the real magnet for Englishmen was the ancient University of Montpellier. Possessor of the first botanical garden to be established in France (given by the tolerant Henry IV in 1596), its reputation for fearless inquiry had been long sustained by its medical school, where bodies had been dissected since 1376. Here Rabelais had once taught and Nostradamus had been a student. Such was its impact on English travellers in search of health that most English 'resorts' adopted the name for one of their streets. Indeed a modern motorist might well find himself driving along Montpellier Street in present day Bath, Brighton, Cheltenham or even Brompton (Austen-Leigh, 1943, 125).

French graduates of Montpellier were active in England too. After a brush with the College of Physicians in Paris, Theodore Mayerne came to London and was knighted in 1624. With yet another Frenchman, Gideon Laune, maker of the famous pills, he worked for the enhancement of the professional status of the Apothecaries (the ancestors of our modern general practitioners), by securing their separation from the Grocers in 1617. He did the same for the Distillers some years later. With another Huguenot he helped produce the first English *Pharmacopoeia*. A tireless experimentalist and annotator (twenty three volumes of his clinical notes are in the British Museum today), he is credited with the formula for the oil still used in royal coronations (Scouloudi, 1940, 301ff).

Other French refugees kept themselves alive in England by writing and teaching. By tongue and pen Peter de

Ploiche, John Véron, G. W. de la Mothe, Pierre Erondelle, Jean de Grave, C. Indupas, Gabriel Dugrès and Claude Manger kept the French language very much alive, helped by ideological sympathies and commercial affinities (Foster Watson, 1909–11, 395–442).

The 'courtly academies' and the grand tour

To English Protestants, Huguenot academies like Saumur, Montpellier, Nîmes, Montauban, Die, Sedan, Orthez (suppressed in 1670) and Geneva proved so attractive that sometimes they stayed there to teach. At Geneva one could not only acquire a purer French than in most of the provinces of France (Lambley, 1920, 233), but one could learn to ride. The English Catholic travellers in turn might visit the universities of Rheims and Douai, where a long list of English graduates is extant (Cardon, 1892), or Paris, Louvain, Cambrai, St. Omer and Arras, where special English seminaries were established following the outlawing of Catholic schools in England.

Both Catholics and Protestants, however, liked riding. This with dancing, fencing and other polite accomplishments, was the especial forte of 'courtly' academies, where private tutors offset the universities' excessive preoccupation with theology. Attempts to establish similar institutions in England by Sir Francis Kynaston (in 1635), Sir Balthasar Gerbier (in 1649) and others prompted Richard Brome's play *New Academy* (1658). Brome had earlier satirised the ladies' passion for things French in *Damoiselle* (1653), a forerunner of numerous such farces.

The revocation of the Edict of Nantes 1681

On hearing that the toleration accorded to Huguenots in France by the Edict of Nantes was to be revoked, Lord Halifax, the tolerant Yorkshire 'trimmer' politician, wrote to his brother, then the British Ambassador in Paris in June 1678:

I am sure we must renounce all good sense if we do not encourage them by all possible invitations. It hath ever been so much my principle that I have wondered at our neglecting a thing we ought to seek; and those that have not zeal enough to endeavour for the preserving of our religion, might have wit enough to do it for the increasing of our trade (de Beer, 1950, 294).

Halifax's words were to be abundantly justified. Not only did his eldest son marry a refugee's daughter five years later, but others dowered England with their gifts. John Chardin, knighted in 1681, the year he came over, became a fellow of the Royal Society and jeweller to the English court. Henry Justel, Louis XIV's secretary, became librarian to St. James Palace; Augustine Courtauld, who came in 1686, became a great silversmith, whilst his great-great-grandson founded the firm that was to manufacture mourning crepes for the Victorians and man-made fibres for our own day (Courtauld, 1924, 125). Others were goldsmiths (Evans, 1933, 496), mapmakers (Tooley, 1952, 479), sculptors (Esdaile, 1949, 254) and bankers. Indeed, when the Bank of England was founded it had seven Huguenot directors.

Amongst other Huguenot families destined to play a leading role in English life were those of Arnold, Beraux, Chenevix, Daubeny, De la Rue, Esdaile, Fourdrinier, Guillebaud, Hertzlet, Jourdain, Kinloch, Le Play, Martineau, Newman, Ogilvie, Pantin, Quartier, Romilly, Sanxay, Thiselton-Dyer, Ully de Laval, Vignolles, Vulliamy, Waddington and Yvonnet. These are only a sample (Wagner, 1926, 287–300), from the great influx of Huguenots which took place after 17 July 1681 when the French Government lowered the age at which the conversion of French children of Protestant parents could be accepted from 12 to 7. Seventeen out of every twenty who took to the sea landed in England (Cunningham, 1897, 229), and it is estimated that, out of these, some 40,000 stayed here.

The steam engine and technical training; the industrial boost

The dissolution of their great intellectual nurseries in France (Sedan was dissolved on 9 July 1681, Saumur on 8 January 1684 and Montauban on 5 March 1684), led them to set about providing for their children in England. Providentially their arrival in England coincided with the relaxation of the difficulties under which English Nonconfirmists had been labouring for the previous twenty years following the passage of the Test and Corporation Acts.

It was at a coffee house in Plymouth that Jacques Sanxay obtained a post as tutor to the family of a Cornish gentleman. His son David founded what was to become the famous preparatory school at Cheam.

So, too, Abel Boyer came to England in 1689 and in the intervals of teaching French to William, Duke of Gloucester, edited an annual register of events, while John Palairet taught three of George II's children. Such refugees contributed to the 'love of gardening and of flowers that now became so characteristic of England' (Trevelyan, 1946, 247).

The father of John Theophilus Desaguliers also started an academy. When he died, Desaguliers went to Hart Hall, Oxford and taught experimental philosophy. Like his fellow countryman, Solomon de Caus, a century before, Desaguliers was especially interested in the potential of the steam engine. The century between them had been bridged by Denis Papin, another émigré and Thomas Savery, a military engineer who had embodied the ideas of Caus in working models, which were finally put to work draining mines by Thomas Newcomen, a Dartmouth ironmonger. After 1717 Desaguliers built or installed seven such engines according to his *Course of Experimental Philosophy* (1734). One of these was for the Czar of Russia.

But Desaguliers was a pioneer in the teaching as well as the application of science. His private apartment was described as having 'more the appearance of a hall of congress than of the auditory of a professor'. The writer was none other than the Prussian ambassador who continued: 'and as we pay him generously, he, in return, spares no pains to entertain us, and to discover to us all the hidden springs of nature'. This was in 1741. The ambassador was then attending twice a week and had 'engaged almost all the foreign ministers to be of the party' (Agnew, 1886, 219–20).

Like other Huguenots, Desaguliers also spoke at the 'penny universities' of the day—the coffee houses. At Slaughter's his fellow countryman Abraham de Moivre was 'one of the attractions of an evening's lounge' (Agnew, 1886, 214) and was often consulted on life assurance rights because of his *Doctrine of Chances, or the Method of Calculating the Probability of Events at Play* (1718). De Moivre also formulated the concept of the normal curve, so important in present-day educational psychology (Kramer, 1951, 183).

By keeping open his contacts with the local French academies (he was awarded a prize by the Academy of Sciences at Bordeaux), and by translating works by the French engineers Marriotte (in 1718) and Vaucauson (in 1742), Desaguliers epitomised the pragmatic and practical approach of the Huguenot exiles in England. His activities, like those of John Dolland, the instrument maker, Stephen Demainbray the electrician, Stephen Rigaud the Savilian professor of geometry at Oxford and Francis Masères, a baron of the exchequer, Anthony Chamier (at whose house Dr. Johnson spent his seventeenth birthday and composed his famous prayer), and Isaac Barré, M.P., justify the observation that the Huguenot emigration was a heaven-sent increment to Britain. One writer sees them as 'lifting England's industrial and technological level and pushing her into the role of industrial leader in the eighteenth and nineteenth century' (Scoville, 1960, 334).

Anglomania and France

For certainly they found life so congenial in England that the King's agent Bonrepaus only succeeded in bribing 507 to return home from January to May 1686. They hymned the delights of English tolerancy for their French countrymen, a tolerance they had done much to secure. For the glorious Revolution of 1688 in England was itself helped by the Revocation of the Edict of Nantes, since 696 Huguenot officers joined the army of William III and other civilians in Holland created 'such a teeming centre of intellectual and religious freedom there' that Locke's philosophy was able to ripen and flower there (Stankiewicz, 1960, 242).

After the English revolution of 1688 appreciative descants on the liberties it conferred on Englishmen were hymned by a virtual procession of Huguenot expositors. Pierre Des Maizeaux, F.R.S., came to England with the third Lord Shaftesbury in 1699 and lived on as the friend of Addison, Collins and David Hume. Béal de Muralt's *Lettres sur les Anglais et les Français et sur les voyages* (1724) 'corrected many of the false ideas the French had of England' (Topazio, 1956, 56). The first Anglo-maniac, the Abbé Prévost, compiled an encyclopaedic publication on matters English—*Le Pour et le Contre*. Voltaire even had to go into hiding after publishing his *Lettres Anglaises et Philosophiques* (1734), which the French government ordered to be burnt by the laymen. Montesquieu endorsed Voltaire's warm praise with his *De l'esprit des lois* (1748), a testimony to the effect upon his philosophy of the experimental, realistic philosophy of Locke.

For Locke provided the Huguenot refugees with the philosophy they embodied: individual conscience as the real arbiter as to what is right and wrong; differences between such individual judgments constituting a necessary and fundamental harmony in society and, lastly, that where action has to be taken as a result of these decisions, it should be decided after full and rational discussion as to the best method. These three Lockean principles were to be the real bases of European democracy as it has been generally understood. This is why Locke made such an enormous appeal to the rationalists of eighteenth century France. Huguenot principles came home behind him to roost.

3

Groups and societies 1570-1790

Incubators of rationalism

Early Huguenot influence has also been detected on Francis Bacon, whose *New Atlantis* (1627) was the blueprint for the Royal Society. For when young Bacon had visited Paris he was influenced by the lectures of Palissy, the Huguenot potter, on geology, chemistry, mineralogy and other aspects of the natural history of the earth (Allbut, 1914, 233). These lectures have been recently described as 'the first of their kind in Paris and perhaps in the world' (Sarton, 1958, 167).

'A kind of Catholic counterblast to Bacon's plan' (Yates, 1947, 287) was launched from the minorite cell of Martin Mersenne. Visited or written to by most of the illustrious savants of Europe, Mersenne dreamt of a superacademy which should embrace all Europe, with constituent members in each nation working to restore the sciences 'from their foundations' and sparing 'no experiment, no labour, no expense' and leaving no aspect of the sciences or their uses unexplored to complete 'the whole Encyclopaedia'.

Though his project came to nothing, continued meetings of like-minded Frenchmen and Englishmen showed how widespread was the desire to communicate discoveries to each other. Other French academies, organised by Mersenne's friends, like Montmor and Mechisidec Thévenot, spread the habit further. Indeed it was later suggested by the famous French scientist, Fontenelle, that 'the English gentlemen who laid the first foundations of the Royal Society had travelled in France, and had visited Messieurs Montmor and Thévenot'.

Aggressive distribution of ideas: offices of address

Whatever the truth of Fontenelle's remark it is certain that the aggressive distribution of new ideas derived from all corners of Europe was first undertaken by a Frenchman, Théophraste Renaudot. In 1612 he established with royal support an 'office and register of addresses'. This was a combination of advertising agency and commercial exchange. Much later he issued a bi-weekly *Gazette*, beginning on 30 May 1631, which carried news of events in France, England, Ireland and Scotland, from correspondents in these countries. Many English periodicals were modelled upon, and took much of their foreign news from, this *Gazette*. The Oxford *Gazette* of 1665, and later the London *Gazette*, even took their titles (T.L.S. 1921, 43).

Such an 'office of address' was attempted by the man who translated Bacon's essays into French, Sir Arthur Gorges, but he failed. During the Commonwealth, private establishments seem to have got under way under Samuel Speed and Henry Robinson. But more interesting are the attempts of Samuel Hartlib to secure a state sponsored office, the purpose of which was to be, according to his associate John Dury, the 'accommodation of the poor, trade, commerce and bargains for profit; actions proceeding from all relations of persons to each other in all estates and conditions of life, and all ingenuities and matters of delight unto the mind in all virtues and rare objects'. Dury wanted Samuel Hartlib appointed as Superintendent-General. This office was also to 'serve for advice in rectifying schools and reforming Colleges' : an essential basis in the great campaign carried out by both men in England at that time. Hartlib especially was interested in an Office of Address for Communications 'with a faire or spacious house for the purpose, which may also serve as an Exchange or Center of all Schollars and Men of Parts'. Hartlib's most recent biographer wrote 'There is not the slightest doubt that the model for the Office of Address was Théophraste Renaudot's Bureau d'Adresse in France' (Turnbull, 1947, 80). The non-establishment of this office by Parliament, however, only intensified Hartlib's personal discharge of its functions. 'He setteth more men a worke' wrote Dury, 'both within and without Great Britain, than perhaps ever any man did of his rank and position'. His known correspondents run to hundreds, and in the period from 1641 to 1660, his papers (which I have seen) teem with suggestions on every conceivable topic, from engines to medicaments, new pedagogic devices to colonial matters. His activities were helped by intermittent grants from Parliament and were so valuable that he was asked to attend Cromwell once a week 'to acquaint his highness with affairs'.

Scientific journals

For the most significant aspect of Renaudot's activities was to start at his 'Bureau d'Adresse' in Paris, a number of conferences where those interested in natural philosophy could meet together to discuss subjects announced beforehand in his *Feuilles du Bureau d'Adresse*. Their discussions were later published, a practice which led to the *Comptes Rendus* of French learned societies. A correspondent in the *Times Literary Supplement* thought it 'possible' that Renaudot's example might have had something to do with the origin of the Royal Society in London (*T.L.S.*, 1921, 44).

Certainly the Royal Society were stimulated to issue

their famous *Philosophical Transactions* as a result of the issue of the *Journal des Sçavans* founded by the encyclopedically minded Denis de Sallo on 5 January 1665. Their *Philosophical Transactions*, first published on 6 March 1665, was however wholly concerned with the publication of new work, whilst the *Journal des Sçavans* was not. That was to be reserved for the *Histoire et Mémoies* of the French Academy of Science, begun after 1700.

English versions of the work done by the French academicians were also provided by John Chamberlayne, F.R.S.—whose interests ranged from translating French works on the making of coffee (in 1685) to Fontanelle's *Lives of the French Philosophers* (1721). He died, aptly enough, in Petty France—now York Street. Even more significantly, the free-thinker Ephraim Chambers, F.R.S. not only translated the most important papers of the Academy—helped by John Martyn, F.R.S., Professor of Botany at Cambridge, but visited France (*Gentleman's Magazine* vii, 314, 351). His activities were sympathetically encouraged by a rising young English publisher—Thomas Longman, whose firm now is one of the major publishing houses in England.

Anglo-French encyclopaedias

Chambers represents an interesting example of the two-way influence prevailing at this time. His *Cyclopaedia* (1728) excited great interest in France and was to have been published there. Instead it inspired Diderot and D'Alembert to embark on their own *Encyclopédie*.

This, from its first volume in 1751, so interpreted Nature as 'the facts of experience' that it was attacked by the Church and the Jesuits. The author of some of the theological articles was deprived of his licence to preach, and the publication of a second volume was forbidden by the French Government. Six further annual volumes provided such provocation that the French public prosecutor stepped in and forbade both the publication of any more volumes, and the sale of those already printed.

To improve on the French *Encyclopédie*, an engraver, a printer and a scholar in Edinburgh decided to issue an *Encyclopaedia Britannica* in a hundred parts, at 6d. a part. Beginning in 1768 and completed in 1771 this ran to a second edition by 1784, which expanded the original three volumes to ten. A third in 1797 carried them to eighteen, and a fourth in 1810 carried them to twenty. It was this which, in the dedication, described the French *Encyclopédie* as 'accused, and justly accused, of having disseminated far and wide the seeds of anarchy and atheism' and expressed the hopes that the *Britannica* would 'combat the tendency of that pestifarous work'.

The secularising ethic of education

The theme of these French *encyclopédistes* was that the only effective moralising agents were secular laws and secular education. Here Helvétius marks a new phase in social thought. He asked for a system of public education in publicly-controlled schools under secular teachers, a theme to be elaborated later by La Chalotais. Both deprecated the influence of clergy who 'being suspended between heaven and earth' were better employed as 'warders of fools' rather than 'teachers of intelligent men' (Cumming, 1955, 162).

Education and environment now emerged as the tempering determinants of the appetites. Locke's suggestion that only experience incised the virgin tablets of the human mind was endorsed by Helvétius as literally true. Indeed he considered education could overcome a bad environment and enable it to be modified. More education, less crime: 'if crimes crush nations, it is only through the effects of ignorance'.

After reading *De l'Ésprit* in 1769, the English utili-

tarian Jeremy Bentham was seized of the idea of 'maxi-
mising felicity' by a judicious combination of the arts
and sciences: a project he gnawed at for forty years,
ultimately producing, in *Chrestomathia*, such a
classification.

Such ideas were flexed and exercised in the salons of
Paris, by a cross-section of intellectuals, self-made and
well-born men in some of the wittiest dialogue of which
history has record. This passion for talking, described by
Harold Nicolson as 'so alarming a factor in French social
life' had, as he saw, several valuable results: 'it sharpened
wits; it spread ideas; and it did more than all the candles
of Versailles to convince awed foreigners that France
was indeed the centre of the civilised world'. (Nicolson,
1960, 216). The premium put on wit spiced with malice
is not unlike the atmosphere of contemporary Oxford
and may indeed have contributed to it.

Of many Englishmen who frequented these salons
the best known was 'that cold and false-hearted Frenchi-
fied coxcomb' (as Wordsworth called him)—Horace
Walpole.

Of the myriad other groups that existed, the 'Club de
l'Entresol' is worth mention. This revolved round the
Abbé de St. Pierre and discussed an international court
for the settlement of disputes and a reformed spelling,
looking to the elimination of ignorance and therefore
prejudice and the attainment of complete happiness.
From these discussions came the Abbé's *Projet de Paix
Perpetuelle* (1713). A later group met for over forty years
at the hospitable table of Baron D'Holbach every Thursday and was known to the encyclopaedists as 'the day
of the Synagogue' (Topazio, 1956, 18). Most Englishmen
of consequence visited him: Gibbon, Wilkes, Sterne,
Garrick, and Priestley.

Chemistry

Priestley was a cultural liaison officer in himself, for his interests transcended mere preoccupation with chemistry, a field which by general consent he share the command at that time with leading Frenchmen like Lavoisier.

For French chemists commanded especial respect in England during the eighteenth century. So much so that when elected to the Chair in the subject at Cambridge in 1764, Richard Watson 'sent immediately' after his election 'for an operator to Paris', since, by his own confession he 'knew nothing at all of chemistry, had never read a syllable on the subject; nor seen a simple experiment in it'. The operator did so well that in fourteen months Watson was able to 'read a course of chemical lectures to a very full audience'.

Such Anglo-French interchange of ideas had been going on for at least a century and a half, activated by the formation of groups like the one to which Priestley, Darwin and Watt belonged: the Lunar Society. The Lunar Society, like many other such groups in France and England were closely linked with the Freemasons, themselves a group that owed much to the Huguenot refugee, J. T. Desaguliers. When Darwin started another group in Derby, and wrote to his Birmingham friends expressing the hope that 'like the freemason societies, we might sometime make your society a visit', he was speaking in a contemporary vein. For the freemasons' lodges were ports of call for men of goodwill in both countries where intellectual stimulus and refreshment were available, secure from the persecutions of suspicious governments.

France 'by one master stroke of policy' might 'almost depopulate this great and flourishing kingdom'. So, in his *Essay on the First Principles of Government* (1768), Priestley saw that 'master stroke' would be toleration. Priestley shared Watson's admiration for French chemists and after going to Paris with Lord Shelburne in 1774 he returned—according to his friend Theophilus Lindsey—a much improved man, for having met Lavoisier and other French men of science like Monsieur Trudaine in their laboratories. Ten years later he was elected to the Paris Academy of Science. Priestley's Francophile learnings were so well-known that he was hounded out of Birmingham when the Revolution broke out, his laboratory destroyed and his friends menaced. It was suggested by the great ironmaster John Wilkinson (who invested £5,000 for him in the French funds) that he migrate to France. The French wished this too, and on 4 October 1791 offered him a vacant monastery near Toulouse in which to do his scientific work. He was made (together with Jeremy Bentham, William Wilberforce and Tom Paine) an honorary French citizen as well as a member of the National Convention. But he chose to go to America.

This Francophile patron, Wilkinson, set up ironworks near Nantes in 1777 in addition to his works and warehouses in Staffordshire, South Wales, Cornwall and London, and even issued his own coinage and notes, modelled on the *monnaies de confiance* issued in France.

The perils of Francophilia

In England Francophilia was increasingly becoming a sign of mere degeneracy. Travel to the continent might breed civility but, as Locke acknowledged, it was 'dearly paid for; and that Irreligion and even Atheism, were, by mistake, packed up with their other curiosities' (Brauer, 1959, 180). Later, on 2 December 1756, *The World* was complaining that 'the majority of our young travellers return home entirely divested of the religion of their country, without having acquired any new one in its place'.

Side by side with this was the steady growth of prejudice against the French. It is mirrored in the world of letters. Addison reported that 'amongst the many honest prejudices naturally cleaving to the heart of a true Englishman was the conviction that one Englishman could beat three Frenchmen' (*Spectator*, 1712, No. 383).

Dr. Johnson, himself not the one to talk, referred to the 'garrulous French' (Boswell, *Life* IV, 1780) implying that they did nothing but talk, and that too quickly.

An indefatigable translator of all things French, including the works of Voltaire, Rousseau and Montesquieu, set a new note with his *Grand Tour* (1749). This was Thomas Nugent, who stressed what could be learned from the country in a positive way. But prejudice, at a time when England and France were in a state of almost continuous war, died hard. Poor Oliver Goldsmith was arrested three years later suspected of being a French recruiting agent.

This debate on the quality of the French reverberated. Going abroad for his health the novelist-surgeon Tobias Smollett made his way to Montpellier. Here he met Laurence Sterne, also in search of health, whose appetite for things French had been whetted by a romantic correspondence with a young French girl at York. Sterne's own *Sentimental Journey through France and Italy* (1768) proved a much needed antidote to Smollett's own cantankerous account of things French, and was a great favourite.

'I left London,' Sterne tells us, 'with so much precipitation that it never enter'd my mind that we were at war with France.' His gay and human perception of the good things of France was to bring down a torrent of Victorian prudery. 'There is not a page of Sterne's writing,' wrote Thackeray, 'but has something that were better away, a latent corruption—a hint as of an impure presence.'

For watching French peasants dancing, Sterne thought he saw 'Religion mixing in'. This daring fusion of religion and pleasure was to be utterly alien from Victorian morals, and it is only in this century that we can be offended not by Sterne's immorality but his sentimentality (Wolf, 1938, 84).

4

The cult of Rousseau

Émile and the soteriology of education

Schools acquired, for the first time, a more critical place
in the future development of society as a result of the
discussions of these groups. Their revolutionary hopes
and psychological theories about the improvement of
society focussed on redemption through education of the
young. Education became a means whereby the state
could ensure that free-born man should never be fettered
by the chains of ignorance. Theological assumptions
about original sin, grace and suffering were discarded and
the so-called contract between rulers and ruled was
sharply questioned by perhaps the best known member
of some of these groups, J. J. Rousseau. From his own
studies in natural history Rousseau cast doubt on the
Lockean idea that a child's mind could be imprinted
by adults to conform to given patterns. Rather, he saw
each child endowed with a nature of its own, varying
according to sex, age and bent. He worked this out in
Émile (1762), the story of a boy taken away from his
home to the seclusion of a village. The tutor (Rousseau
mythologised) allows him complete freedom, within a
protective pale. Having acquired by the age of two, the
capacity to eat, walk and talk, the child then goes on
to acquire the mastery of the five senses up to the age

of twelve. At twelve the child becomes a virtual Robinson Crusoe, discovering physics, geography, astronomy, whilst at the same time discovering himself. This self discovery is enhanced, at fifteen by his sexual development, his relations to others. When mature he leaves the village to find a mate.

Though *Émile* emphasised that the absence of external restraints is necessary to the development of the child, Rousseau nevertheless argued, in his article 'Political Economy' in the *Encyclopédie* (1755) that children should be reared by the State to ensure their conformity to the 'general Will' of the community.

The second blow, this time in the political sphere, was also struck in 1762 by Rousseau when he investigated the profit and loss account on the imaginary contract of free and happy natural man with society in his *Du Contrat Social*.

Both books evoked the same persecutory mania as the ideas of the Huguenots had done. So Rousseau fled, first to Geneva, then to England where David Hume looked after him for a year at Wootton, Derbyshire. Though he returned to France in 1767 he left many disciples, notably Thomas Day.

Thomas Day's Sandford and Merton

Day was the first English martyr to the new faith in Rousseau for his desire not to interfere with nature led him to ride an unbroken colt—with fatal consequences. But he was in late middle age then. As a young man he found every page of *Émile* big with important truth. The more he read, the more he admired. He considered *Émile* second only to the Bible. 'Excellent Rousseau', he wrote. 'First of human kind! Behold a system, which, preserving to man all the faculties and the excellences and the liberty of his nature, preserves a *medium* between the brutality and ignorance of a savage and the corruptions of society' (Sadler, 1928, 9).

No revolution is possible without a crank, and Day was an effective one. He adopted two girls, an eleven year old blonde from Shrewsbury and a brunette from London. His idea was to educate them to see which would prove the best wife. The latter proved so stupid that he had to apprentice her to a shopkeeer, whilst the former, after a further course of education at Lichfield and a board-school at Sutton Coldfield, married his friend Bicknell, a lawyer. Nor should we be surprised. Day trained her to bear pain by dropping sealing-wax on her arm, and to be courageous by firing a pistol at her petticoats.

Having lost his two wards he turned to two sisters, but lost them too—to his friend Edgeworth, who married each in turn. So Day married a Miss Esther Milnes of Wakefield, with whom he ran the village of Anninglsey, near Ottershaw in Surrey. Here he tried his theories on other young girls, including Edgeworth's daughter Maria, whom he used to dose daily with Tar-water to cure inflammation of her eyes.

Day's enthusiasm for the noble savage and aversion to the so-called corruptions of luxurious society frightened most of his friends away. So in retirement near Ottershaw in Surrey he spent his time farming and studying mechanics and chemistry. His belief that if he was kind to men that they would be kind to him even extended to *not* training horses. As already mentioned, it killed him, for he died riding an unbroken colt.

Richard Lovell Edgeworth and child study

Day's legacy, his novel, *Sandford and Merton*, was originally meant as a short story to be inserted in some stories of his friend Richard Lovell Edgeworth, on whom *Émile* had made 'a great impression'. So he determined to let the mind of his young son be left 'as much as possible to the education of nature and accident'. He was then twenty-three, and his son, three. The effects on the son were startling. According to his father, he went about without stockings or sleeves 'in a jacket and trowsers which were at that time novel and extraordinary'. Not only was he hardy, having 'all the virtues of a child bred in the hut of a savage' but he had 'all the knowledge of *things* which could be well acquired at an early age by a boy bred in a civilised society' (Edgeworth, 1821, i, 221). Like many modern American children reared on permissive, child-centred techniques, 'he had less knowledge of books than children half his age', but, wrote the father, 'of mechanics he had a clearer conception, and in the application of what he knew more invention than any child I had then seen'.

When the boy was five, an ex-army officer, James Keir came to stay with his father in order to translate from the French P. J. Macquer's *Dictionary of Chemistry*. Published three years before, Macquer's was the first chemical dictionary and Keir's translation and own notes and additions made it so valuable that on the strength of them Keir took up glass making. Later with the help of one of his former army friends he set up a chemical works at Tipton which became as large as any in England. This marked the emergence of the British Alkali Industry (Padley, 1951, 64).

No one knew better than Keir how much chemistry owed to the French, especially in the field of 'gases', a term which he introduced into England in place of 'elastic fluids' or 'airs'. From Jean Rey in 1630, van Helmont, Nollet, De Luc, Rey and Lavoisier, this interchange of new ideas with English chemists continued, and Keir's *Treatise on the Various Kinds of Permanently Elastic Fluids or Gases* said so in 1777.

Edgeworth himself was interested in technology rather than science, tinkering with innovations like telegraphy, caterpillar traction and shorthand. He also subjected his numerous children to the first pioneer child study of the age, and with the help of his kindly, energetic and capable eldest daughter Maria, published the results in *Practical Education* (1798). Based on an actual record, initiated by the second Mrs. Edgeworth twenty-two years before, it was not only a register of observations, but it also caught up and made current other contemporary ideas.

Learning, in Edgeworth eyes, was a very active process, and if the spontaneity of the play impulse was checked, provoked mischief of a more serious kind. It remained for Froebel to restate this with such effectiveness that it is now a commonplace. To Maria's sixteen chapters (mainly philosophical), her father added six of his own composition (mainly practical), while her half-brother Lovell (sixth in the family) contributed one on the teaching of chemistry. Only one chapter was written by both father and daughter—that on 'Tasks'. The question of religion was ignored: indeed their silence on the question provoked the reproaches of their French translator Pictet, some three years later. Nor did fairy tales fit into the Edgeworth scheme of things. 'Why should the mind be filled with fantastic visions instead of useful knowledge? asked Maria. The only fantasy Maria would admit was Darwinian—*Practical Education* was published seven years after Erasmus Darwin's *Botanical Garden* and caught some of its mechanophilic élan. Her fairy stories were also woven around inventors and manufacturers as the very title of one, *Rosanna, the Manufacturer and Other Tales* indicates. No wonder Lord Byron groaned that 'Miss Edgeworth's Cupid must be a presbyterian'.

The Rev. David Williams and the new morality

A third experiment was undertaken with children in 1773 by the Rev. David Williams, a dissenting minister, who in the following year harboured Benjamin Franklin who was much interested in the way Williams taught arithmetic. With Franklin he drew up a liturgy on the *Univer-*

sal Principles of Religion and Morality (1776): a significant document which served as the basis for a new chapel he opened in Margaret Square, Cavendish Street, subsequently transferring his efforts to a Charing Cross Coffee House. He preached the need for toleration. Lampooned as 'Orpheus, Priest of Nature' in 1781 Williams was suspected of turning his hearers to atheism. Perhaps this was when he translated some of Voltaire's writings and was active in the cause for parliamentary reform. He was subsequently made a French citizen in the early stages of the revolution. During the Revolutionary Wars he was believed to have served as an unofficial emissary in 1802.

Rousseau's cry 'Back to Nature' was, according to Frank Smith (1931, 126), 'the ultimate source of the spate of children's books that came at the end of the eighteenth century.' Refracted at second or third hand, it was echoed by Madame de Genlis, who came to England as an émigré in 1791. She was the author of an *Émile*-type tract, *Adèle et Théodore* (1782).

The revisionists: Pestalozzi

Having tried to apply the ideas in *Émile* to the education of his own son, J. H. Pestalozzi was dissatisfied with the result. He wrote, when the boy was four, 'we must bring together what Rousseau has separated. The child has much necessary and seemingly meaningless labour in preparing for the duties, conventions and accomplishments of social life.' So Pestalozzi started at Stanz, an institution which, whilst recognising the importance of appealing to the five senses of children, nevertheless kept the teacher as 'benevolent superintendent of such appeals'. Later he went to Yverdun where he trained teachers for the Prussian Government.

Pestalozzi had numerous English visitors, Andrew Bell, initiator of the 'Madras' or 'monitorial' method of teaching and ideologue of the National Society for Educating the Poor in the Principles of the Church of England; Dr. Charles Mayo, who in 1822 was to return and establish a Pestalozzian school at Cheam, and later, the Home and Colonial School Society; Robert Owen, who was pioneer of infant education at New Lanark; and Dr. James Kay who, as the first secretary of the embryo of what is now the Department of Education and Science, was vastly impressed.

It was through Pestalozzian disciples that progressive ideas were taken to America, whence they were beamed back to England in the middle of the century.

Moniteurs *and monitors*

French *moniteurs* (a still surviving office in the lycées), were envisaged by the French Committee of Public Instruction in 1792. For on its behalf in December of that year F. Lanthenas reporting to the National Convention advocated their adoption as enabling four classes to be taught by one teacher at the same sitting. Moreover, he added, 'the attempts of the most capable children to teach their schoolmates what they themselves know, and to inculcate it upon them, will instruct themselves more effectively than would their master's lessons' (Hippeau, 1881, 294).

This principle was imaginatively and profitably exploited by Joseph Priestley's disciple, Thomas Wright Hill, at a school he founded at Hill Top, Birmingham, in 1802, which bears extended description, not only because of this but because it is a mirror of his ideas.

The 'monitors' in this case were his eldest son Matthew Davenport Hill (then ten years old), his second, Edwin (then nine). His third, Rowland (then seven) was later to join them, followed by Frederic (born that very year) and William Howard (born two years later). Five years later Hill expressed his 'unspeakable pleasure' at finding:

33

that my boys could for a whole week conduct the school, now larger than ever, without assistance from me. In a few years they will not only have the real power, but from age would be entitled to the public confidence.

Matthew was then fifteen. Edwin fourteen, and Rowland twelve years old.

Hill Top became a schoolboy republic, administered, judged and operated by the pupils through a school currency for rewarding and penalising slackness. Fines were levied by a schoolboy court and rewards were earned by voluntary work on models, etching, versifying or reading. All had a voice in determining what those verdicts should be. Languages were spoken and the throttling hands of death were never asked to grind at grammar.

In the decade following Waterloo Rowland even supplanted his father. Speech Day was superseded by an exhibition. A trigonometrical survey of Birmingham was undertaken. Visits to coal mines and canals were organised. A weekly staff meeting was instituted to discuss 'improvements to be introduced'. Of this Rowland wrote, 'I find the conference a most powerful engine': surely an endorsement of Lunar group therapy. The youngest children learned the school code with the alphabet so that 'school morality' could be 'imbibed with the pupils' earliest letters'. It was Rowland, too, who designed the new buildings at Hazelwood, into which the school moved in 1819. By then he could write: 'a few days ago, without any solicitation, or even a hint on my part, my father took me into partnership: that is to say, all our business since has been carried on under the firm of Thomas Wright Hill and Son'. An account of their work, *Plans for the government and liberal instruction of boys in large numbers, drawn from experience* (1822) was a great success. With F. C. Ruinet, a French language teacher and E. W. Brayley, who specialised in the physical sciences, they built up such a team that after moving to London, where curiously enough they took over the house of John Wilmot, who had been the chairman of the committee set up to look after the French émigrés during the revolution. This was Bruce Castle, Tottenham, which became a mecca for the educationalists of the day.

D

5

French revolutionary Institutions

Émigré Catholics and their schools in England

These émigrés were 10,000 non-juring priests and a number of nobility and gentry who flooded into England for refuge (Greer, 1951, 94). Given assistance by the government and private persons after 1792, they contributed in three ways to English education.

Firstly, they provided what are now the five leading Roman Catholic public schools. The monks of Douai made their way to Ware and Durham, where they founded St. Edmunds and Ushaw. The old 'English' College founded by the exiled Father Robert Parsons three hundred years earlier at St. Omer was given sanctuary in an old Elizabethan mansion in Ribblesdale, Lancashire in 1794. Sixteen years later, as Stonyhurst College, it was occupying a new building. Other exiles from Lorraine and Douai founded Ampleforth (1803) and Downside (1815). These five were to provide for the *élite of* English Catholics, and were recognised, by the charter of the University of London, as enabling boys to proceed for degrees in the days when Catholics were excluded from Oxford and Cambridge.

Secondly, they afforded a living object lesson to Anglicans opposed to the spirit of Jacobinism. The eloquent and voluble Bishop of Rochester cited them as providing as an 'edifying example of patient suffering for conscience sake'. Like the 'Bishop in Petticoats', Hannah More, he deplored radical excess in France against which these émigrés had stumbled, arguing that unless it was kept under control a revolution would take place in England too. He followed up this sermon in the House of Lords in 1793 (also directed against Methodist Sunday Schools as Jacobin nurseries of 'sedition and atheism') by a further outburst against radicalism in his episcopal charge some seven years later.

Thirdly, the son of one of them helped to popularise a new architectural style for educational buildings by building St. Edmunds, Ware, St. Cuthbert's, Ushaw and a later Roman Catholic school, Ratcliffe College in Leicester as well as designing new buildings for Balliol College, Oxford, Jesus College, Cambridge and King Edward VI School, Birmingham. Though Balliol did not materialise from his plans, and his buildings for King Edward VI no longer exist, his influence was decisive. He was A. W. Pugin, many of whose buildings still retain their impact on the eye.

The pro-revolutionary John Anderson and his 'university'

To check the spread of revolutionary ideas in Ireland, the English Government acceded to a petition of the Catholic bishops and by the Maynooth Act of 1795, sanctioned the formation of Maynooth College to train more clergy. This revived the religious divisions in that unhappy country, since four years later a presbyterian petition for a more broadly based university of Ulster was turned down.

Considering what had gone forward in Scotland, perhaps the government should not be blamed. For when the French Revolution broke out the Professor of Natural Philosophy of the University of Glasgow offered a gun he had invented to the French Assembly. The members hung it in their meeting place under the inscription THE GIFT OF SCIENCE TO LIBERTY. The Assembly also adopted the professor's suggestion to disseminate propaganda across Europe by means of fire balloons.

This professor used to lecture every Tuesday and Thursday to the manufacturers and artificers of the City of Glasgow and on his death in 1796 he bequeathed his fine collection of scientific instruments, 'the most valuable in England and perhaps in Europe' (Muir, 1950, 23), to 81 trustees to establish a 'University or Studium Generale, for the Improvement of Human Nature, of Science and of the Country'. It was to be called by his name: 'Anderson's University' to differentiate it from the University of Glasgow. And so from 1796 to 1828 Anderson's Institution had a home, first in George Street, then in John Street. It is now the University of Strathclyde in George Street.

Anderson's Institution helped incubate further experiments in technical education in that the first professor of natural philosophy, Dr. Thomas Garnett, appointed in 1796, delivered several successful series of lectures on the application of science to arts and manufactures before going on to become the first professor at another new foundation, the Royal Institution in London. His successor Dr. George Birkbeck successfully organised a school for mechanics and intended to offer lectures on these subjects for children (Kelly, 1957, 34). But the task of whipping up enthusiasm for this and other courses led him to resign after five years and settle in London. His successor, a chemist, Dr. Andrew Ure, continued the classes but in 1823 they seceded and formed their own mechanics institute, with Birkbeck as patron.

These mechanics institutes had a more direct link with France, in that in October 1823, the editor of *The Mechanics' Magazine* called attention to the *Conservatoire des Arts et Métiers* (founded in 1794) as a place 'where instruction is liberally dispersed by professors appointed and paid by government, on most subjects connected with mechanics'. Without wishing to emulate such state organisation, he cited previous attempts in Glasgow, Edinburgh and Liverpool as evidence that the London mechanics could establish their own institute.

After the London Mechanics Institute took shape, the great French engineer Charles Dupin came to England to see it in operation, though such instruction was already being given in France (Audigane, 1851, 860).

He returned to increase its provision there (Kelly, 1957, 255).

The École Polytechnique *and its Regent Street counterpart*

Technical instruction in England received a more direct stimulus from the establishment in 1794 of the École Polytechnique in Paris. This was the first institution of its kind in the world, the ancestor of the *technische hochschule* of Germany. It also aroused the spirit of envy in England. John Nash produced a scheme for linking Carlton House to Marylebone by a great processional way. 'It will quite eclipse Napoleon,' cried the Prince Regent, whose name it bore—Regent Street. This was to lead into Trafalgar Square where, Nash suggested, all the learned societies should be concentrated. Begun singularly enough when Napoleon was banished to St. Helena, Regent Street was virtually completed by 1828 and Nash was embarking on further enterprises at both ends of it: Cumberland Terrace in Regent's Park to the north and Buckingham Palace in the south.

After Nash died in 1834 William Mountford Nurse developed the north terminal at Regent's Park where he built several terraces and in 1837, a Polytechnic in Regent Street. This he leased to the Polytechnic Institution which had been incorporated by charter in August 1838, the moving spirit of which was the Yorkshire squire-scientist Sir George Cayley. But Cayley and Nurse disagreed about principles so the polytechnic scheme fell to pieces. By 1857 the polytechnic came under the control of a clergyman, the Rev. Joseph Owen whose *Business without Christianity, with Statistics and Facts* had just been published. He virtually anaesthetised it with unction. It died with him in 1870 and when resurrected by Quintin Hogg, was restarted as a boys' club. Only when re-endowed with the proceeds of obsolete London charities and given other financial assistance did it develop on its present lines.

The real revolution: ∂-ism replaces dot-age

The real French revolution in England was in the teaching of mathematics. For the analytical methods of the mathematicians in the Polytechnic—as outlined in the books of the founder, Monge, or professors like Lagrange, Laplace, Poisson, Fourier and Legendre—dethroned the century old dominance of Newton's calculus.

The impulse was soon felt in Newton's own university of Cambridge when as early as 1803, the ideas of Lagrange were subjected to critical analysis by Robert Woodhouse. By so doing, wrote his biographer, 'he rendered his general support of the system far more weighty than if he appeared to embrace it as a blind partisan'. (*D.N.B.*, 1948, lxii, 402). Six years later his *Elements of Trigonometry* (1809) 'more than any other contributed to revolutionise the mathematical studies of this country' by preparing the way for the introduction of the differential calculus. His 'disciples' founded the Cambridge Analytical Society in 1812 to substitute Leibnizian notation in the calculus ($\partial y/\partial x$) for Newtonian ($\dot{y}$ and $\ddot{y}$): as Charles Babbage said 'pure ∂-ism as opposed to the *dot*-age of the university'. Babbage, who campaigned vigorously for the support of science in England, pointed out that there was 'no single term' to describe its cultivators except the French word *savant* (Cardwell, 1957, 60).

As a participant in this revolution (who later retired to Paris) Dionysius Lardner described these French textbooks as providing the impulse for mathematics to leap the 'chasm of a hundred years'. For Lardner witnessed the changes effected in Trinity College, Dublin, by the Professor of Mathematics, who 'conceived and executed the most important and rapid revolution ever effected in the academic studies of a university' (McConnell 1943, 76). Amongst those who profited by the changes in Dublin was Sir William Rown Hamilton, who as a sixteen year old undergraduate detected an error of reasoning in Laplace's *Mécanique Céleste*, and went on to outline a general method of dynamics and virtually created the calculus of vectors. For this he was known as 'the Irish Lagrange'.

Charles Babbage himself extended the work of the French physicist Arago in magnetism. He then turned to Pascal's work on calculating machines, devoting thirty-seven years of his life to building an 'analytical engine' based on the punched card system devised by the French engineer Jacquard for use in looms.

The Conservatoire des Arts et Métiers

Babbage's debt to Jacquard illustrates the influence of yet another French institution—the museum of technology. For Jacquard himself owed the idea of his silk weaver's loom to such a collection that had been originally amassed by Jacques de Vaucanson for educational purposes in order to train his workmen. On Vaucanson's death in 1782 his collection went to Louis XVI and twelve years later the French Convention took it over as the nucleus of a museum. Housed in an old Benedictine priory in St. Martin-des-Champs, from 1799 onwards, the *Conservatoire des Arts et Métiers* became a virtual industrial university as well as a museum of science and technology.

'It seems highly probable,' wrote Professor Wolf, 'that the decree of the Convention in 1794, to establish the *Conservatoire*, had something to do with the proposal made by Count Rumford, two years later, for the creation of something similar in London' (Wolf, 1938, 42). This 'something similar' was the Royal Institution in Albemarle Street.

This became, not so much an industrial university, as a scientific club for upper-class Londoners 'where lectures could be heard and the latest scientific periodicals read in comfort' (Sparrow, 1964, 131).

The concept of the 'normal' school

Another revolutionary institution was the 'normal school' or *école normale*, founded in 1794 for the training of secondary school teachers. Suppressed in the following years it was revived after the Imperial University was established in 1808. The *aggrégation* was instituted, and voluntary periods of practice teaching. A college for primary teachers followed in 1811, taking pupils from 16 upwards, for four years. By 1833, France possessed seven such schools, mainly offering two-year courses. They evoked admiration, especially in Scotland. Professor J. Pillans considered them in the *Edinburgh Review* and another Scotsman appropriated the name 'normal' for the seminary he established in Glasgow in 1837. The rector's post attracted the interest of Thomas Carlyle who thought he would like 'to superintend the practical working of the system pursued in the Model Schools, and to superintend and train the Normal Students both in the theory and in the art of teaching and training'. Though he didn't get the post, the one who did spent several preparatory months in France and Germany. This Glasgow normal school is generally acknowledged to be 'the first of the training colleges to attempt to devise a technique of training' (Rich, 1933, 38).

The idea of the French *brevet de capacité*—or certificate for teachers—was canvassed by the Select Committee on Education in 1835, but it was left to Dr. James Kay to found the Battersea Normal School and institute the English pupil teacher system in 1846.

The rise of professional training

Five other types of professional school, pioneered in France, were emulated in England. The construction of roads and canals needed qualified engineers and here France had led Europe by founding the École des Ports et Chausées in 1747, under Jean Perronet. A similar need for military engineers led to the foundation of the École de Génie Militaire in the following year. The growing importance of transport and the need to get more out of horses led to the foundation of the first veterinary school in Europe in 1761. A pioneer agricultural school in the same place was founded in 1785. Lastly, a school of mines, on the German model, was founded in France in 1783.

All five types received state aid either in the form of direct foundation grants or scholarships for students. But only when their value had been proved in a war against Britain were they emulated. Counterparts of the *École des Ponts et Chaussées* and the *École Militaire* were provided by governmental military schools at High Wycombe (1799), Great Marlow (1804) and the private college at Addiscombe established in 1809 by the East India Company to train engineers. A Frenchman founded the first English veterinary college in 1792, whilst a former student at Montpellier, John Sibthorp, endowed a chair of rural economy at Oxford which bore his name. It needed the findings of N. T. de Saussure on plant nutrition, of Sir Humphrey Davy on agricultural chemistry and Liebig's paper on organic chemistry before a local agricultural society established a proper agricultural college at Cirencester in 1845. Yet another six years had to pass before a government School of Mines and Science applied to the Arts was founded.

Many Englishmen deplored with Vicesimus Knox (a former headmaster of Tonbridge School), that 'the sciences which Bonaparte encouraged (chiefly for the sake of raising engineers, gunners, surgeons, and all other persons who assist in sieges and works of slaughter), are becoming in England the fashionable study to the exclusion, or at least the comparative neglect, of polite literature'.

Travellers' tales

Reports of these French innovations were made by Sir John Carr and Francis Blagdon, two of some 2,000—some say 12,000—Englishmen who visited France in the brief interlude following the Peace of Amiens in 1802 (Alger, 1904, 25). Carr was a Devonshire gentleman of means, whose travels excited considerable interest when published. Introduced to the man who first employed hydrogen to fill balloons, Jacques Charles, later Professor of Physics at the *École des Arts et Métiers*, he inspected his 'immense electrical machines'. Even more thoroughly, Francis Blagdon, a journalist familiar with France before the revolution, described the place which science had attained in French public esteem by providing the steel, iron, saltpetre and gunpowder that enabled the French to win their victories and emancipate themselves from dependence on other nations: 'Science,' wrote Blagdon, was 'nearly allied to pride and national interest, while literature concerns only the vanity and interest of a few individuals.'

At the *Polytechnique*, the *Conservatoire des Arts et Métiers*, the *Musée des Mines* and the *Jardin des Plantes*, Blagdon found great stimulus and stressed the number of public lectures offered there. Especially was he impressed with the *Institut* (see Chapter 8) and the Hospitals where there were, thanks to government contribution, many extra beds. He dilated on the importance of the metric system and the new administrative structure.

Yet another new institution which impressed him was the *Bibliothèque Nationale*. Created by the confiscation of the Royal Library and augmented by the libraries of émigrés and monasteries, and from the conquest of Holland, Germany and Belgium, it was now a superb national collection calculated to excite the envy of any bibliophile; especially since, within its precincts, one could learn Oriental Languages at a special school established under the *Conservateur* of Antiques and Medals there.

One who has studied these published travellers' reports concludes that 'other English visitors of the period were similarly struck by the intelligent interest shown by the Parisian crowd at the Louvre, the *Jardin des Plantes* etc. . . . [and] occasionally remark upon the behaviour and comments in the course of sight-seeing of some of their own countrymen, which did not always compare favourably' (Maxwell, 1932, 236).

By 1814 some other English travellers were even more explicit. Morris Birkbeck for instance did 'not believe that there is among the French a feeling of jealousy towards us, a sentiment of national rivalship such as I am sorry to see cherished on this side of the water. They have no idea of the English and French being natural foes; the animosity which has been said to prevail between the two nations they refer exclusively to the Governments'. To Birkbeck it seemed that 'forty million of civilised people in the two countries' were 'the dupes of a wretched and disgraceful policy, by which governments foment perpetual rivalship and war, under the hackneyed plea of supporting social order and religion!'

Birkbeck, despairing of his native England, soon emigrated to America. Babbage, who did not, remained at home. We have already noted (*supra* page 40) that Babbage was a supporter of French mathematics. He was also a supporter of the meritocratic nature of French science, which elicited from him some melancholy *Reflections on the Decline of Sciences in England* (1830). In this he brooded on the fact that the French scientist was adequately rewarded, whereas his British counterpart was not. One had the *École Polytechnique* and the *École Normale*, the other had not—only the faint prospect of an appointment at the Board of Longitude. Otherwise Babbage wrote, he had 'no situations in the state . . . no

45

situations in society to which hope can point, to cheer him in his laborious path'.

To this particular argument we shall return. Meanwhile let us conclude by looking at the impact of the revolution on the periphery of British education.

The Imperial University of 1808, and its influence on Ireland and Wales

The shilling a day allowed to Revolutionary émigrés by the English Government was not enough for the twenty-five year old Vicomte de Chateaubriand. So he took a teaching post at Bungay in Suffolk, where he staved off boredom by writing and flirting with the parson's wife and daughter. Returning to London he announced his rejection of Christianity in his *Essay on Revolution* (1797). This earned him an appointment to the embassy of Rome, together with the friendship of Louis Fontanes, the journalist. Much later, Chateaubriand was to return to London as French ambassador—this time not in dingy garrets in Holborn and Marylebone, but the comfort of 4 Portland Place.

Fontanes became the head of the state system of secondary and higher education known as the *Université impériale* and later as the *Université de France*. By a decree of 17 March 1808 France was divided into regional *académies* whose respective *recteurs* were both vice-chancellors and directors of education. As its head and highest ranking official the first *Grand-Maître de l'université*, Fontanes used his power to appoint as an inspector of the University of Paris a friend of Chateaubriand, Joseph Joubert. Joubert was also a moralist who profoundly influenced Matthew Arnold, who was later to argue for establishing a modified version of the Imperial University in the shape of faculties in eight or ten large towns controlled by a minister of education advised by a 'Superior Council of Public Instruction' which appointed professors. These eight or ten faculties were, as in France, not to examine for, or award, degrees; that was to be reserved for the nuclear or central university complex of Oxford, Cambridge and London.

As a secular system controlled from the centre, the concept of the Imperial University also animated the establishment in 1845 of the Queen's Colleges at Belfast, Cork and Galway (Culler, 1955, 125). These were to be constituent members of the non-sectarian federated, Queen's University of Ireland. Attacked as 'godless' by the M.P. for Oxford, the so-called Queen's Colleges were also opposed by the Irish Catholic Bishops, who decided to establish a Catholic University of Ireland in Dublin. Appointed as rector of this Dublin University, Newman tried to Christianise the Imperial University idea, by trying to show Ireland as the 'centre of the Catholicism of the English tongue with Great Britain, Malta (perhaps Turkey or Egypt), and India, on one side of it, and North America and Australia on the other' (Newman, 1896, 49). But the concept was too euphoric. 'Who in his senses,' said one convert, 'would send his children to a province at a distance for the completion of education? . . . It is a joke. An Imperial University in Ireland is an absurdity' (Culler, 1955, 169).

But Newman never went as far as some of his contemporary Catholics in France, like *l'Univers*, which championed the view that the teaching of the classics should be abolished as they diffused a pagan ethic which had prepared the way for the French revolution. Newman thought this view 'startling' and rejected it (Culler, 1955, 264).

Meanwhile Queen's Colleges were also being mooted for Wales. In 1848 and again in 1854 schemes were launched to this end. The prime mover of the second attempt was Hugh Owen, who was also anxious to promote the Eisteddfod. He would, he said, 'never rest until the Welsh educational appliances have been perfected'; a declaration which a recent writer described as 'a fine, clanking sentence, which would have warmed the heart of Auguste Comte' (Williams, 1964, 73). Indeed, it was at the Eisteddfod of 1863 that the movement to found a scientific, vocationally-oriented examining university was launched, which culminated in the establishment of University College, Aberystwyth in 1872. After Cardiff and Bangor had been added in 1883 and 1884 respectively a federal university was duly established.

The crown of the edifice: the Institut

The French educational system was crowned by the *Institut National de France*. This embodied four academies: the Academie des Sciences, the pre-revolutionary Académie française, the Académies of Painting and Sculpture and of Inscriptions and Medals. A fifth, the Academy of Moral and Political Sciences was set up in 1795, abolished in 1803 and refounded in 1832.

Founded in 1795 as 'to record discoveries and improvements in arts and sciences', and remodelled in 1803, 1816 and 1836 the Institut consisted of members of the five academies elected from the best in their five fields. Its members took pride in a ceremonial uniform designed specially for them by Napoleon I. The five constituent academies are autonomous but meet in the same place— the Palace of the Institute, and bestow much-sought-after honours in the form of prizes. It is eminently suited for the award of honours in a democracy.

To a nineteenth century scientist like Sir David Brewster it was 'the noblest and most effective institution that ever was organised for the promotion of science'. He lamented the state of the English societies, which were 'defective in their constitution, limited in their operation, and incapable, from their very nature, of developing, and directing, and rewarding the indigenous talent of the country'. But, argued Brewster, if an *Institut* of Britain were to be set up 'established on the basis of our existing institutions, with a class of resident members enabled to devote themselves wholly to science' he prophesied that 'our universities would then breathe a more vital air. Our science would put forth new energies, and our literature might rise to the high level at which it stands in our sisterland' (Howarth, 1931, 261). But strong opposition from his brother scientists no less than the existence of other mechanisms for awarding 'honours' prevented its further pursuit. Yet the allocation of Burlington House to accommodate some of the leading scientific societies and the establishment in 1902 of the Order of Merit represent, albeit infinitesimally, an appreciation of the principle on which the *Institut* was founded. (See also *infra* p. 73).

6

The soteriology of education

The Catholic reaction

> Return then to your own country, go back to the re-
> ligion of your fathers, and follow it in sincerity of
> heart, and never forsake it; it is very simple and very
> holy; I think there is no other religion upon earth
> whose morality is purer, or other more satisfying to the
> reason.

The advice of the Savoyard Vicar in Rouseau's *Émile*
was taken up by many young men in the early nineteenth
century to whom the rationalism of the Revolution was
unsatisfactory. When coupled to this, Chateaubriand's
Genius of Christianity appeared, many were enabled to
enter the churches with intellectual conviction (Masson,
1916, 272). The priestly injunctions of Lamennais to 'Cathol-
icise liberalism so that society will be reborn' produced in
1830 the journal *L'Avenir* and the *Agence Générale
pour la défense de la liberté religeuse.*

Though condemned by the Pope, these Liberal Catholics
had the ears of reading people. Helped by writers like the
journalist-politician Montalembert, and preachers like
Lacordaire, they championed trade unions, freedom of
association, and social justice, presenting, it was said,
'holy water in a *bonnet rouge*' (Collins, 1923, 29).

Especially did these Liberal Catholics press the need for
schools free of the constricting monopoly of the Napole-

onic University. Even under Napoleon the Church had already created *petits séminaires* which, though ostensibly training priests, became such successful rivals of the *lycées*, that Napoleon decreed in 1811 that there should be only one such *séminaire* in a department, and that it was not to rival the University's *lycée*. After the Restoration this edict was rescinded and the church obtained such a hold on the university that two ordinances were passed in 1828. One forbade Jesuits to teach there, the other limited the number admitted to clerical *séminaires*.

A further revolution brought Guizot to the Ministry of Public Instruction. To secure the church's support for the Orleanist monarchy, and enrol teachers in the army of social disciplinarians, he secured, by his law of 1883, that there should be a primary school in every commune and a training college in every department. When he tried to do this for secondary schools in 1836 his schemes backfired. *L'Écho des Instituteurs*, the teachers' journal founded [and militantly directed by the republican Arsène Meunier] attacked him for playing the teachers into the hands of the church.

Guizot's influence in England

Guizot was much admired in England by those, who, like him, wished to harness the forces of 'Jacobinism'. Thomas Arnold, J. A. Roebuck, Lord Brougham and Matthew Arnold all paid him public tribute at various times, so much so that Guizot told the foreign editor of *The Times*, 'je vis aussi en Angleterre. C'est beaucoup d'avoir deux vies et presque deux patries' (Johnson, 1963, 441). Nor was this admiration confined to his official achievements. Much earlier, from 1811 to 1814, he had founded and edited the *Annales de l'Éducation*, in which he had tentatively floated many common topics for discussion for the rest of the century. Amongst them was the Rousseauist insistence on activity. 'One must try in one's method of teaching,' he wrote (1811, i, 106), 'to make the child an active being who can exercise his growing forces on what he is learning, rather than a passive being placed so as to receive what people want to confer on his memory or thought.'

Another of Guizot's actions that affected England was the social stocktaking he initiated. His dispatch of Victor Cousin to report on public instruction in the German states, attracted the attention of Mrs. Austin (wife of the Professor of Law at London University) who translated it in 1834. Another of Cousin's reports attracted the attention of one of one of the first four very influential factory inspectors, anxious to see that the children they kept out of factories had schools to attend. This inspector, Leonard Horner, saw that it was useless passing factory acts to keep children out of factories unless schools were provided to contain them. Cousin's accounts also stimulated Dr. James Kay (later Sir James Kay-Shuttleworth) to set about visiting the continent so that he could better discharge his duties as the first secretary of a committee appointed to help England's voluntary schools with grants.

Yet another writer drew heavily on Cousin for his most successful *England and the English* (1833). This was the dazzling young writer who was later to be known as Lord Lytton, one of those dashing social commentators who always succeed in England. This nineteenth century Anthony Sampson so stimulated the public that his book raced through three editions in a year. Lytton's book was a brief both for state education and for Babbage's theme : the need to reward scientists. For as he said

> In England the cultivation of science is not a profession. In France, the institutions of the country open a considerable field of ambition to the cultivators of science; in Prussia the range of employments is still wider.

St. Simonians in England

France also provided an object lesson in the soteriology of education : its redemptive component.

As John Stuart Mill wrote

> You are far ahead of us in France—you have only to teach men what is right and they will do it; they are uninformed but they are not prejudiced, and are desirous and eager to learn. Here the great difficulty is to make them desire to learn. They have such an opinion of their own wisdom that they do not think they can learn; and they have too little regard for other people to care much whether they learn or not in things which only interest the nation in general or mankind at large (Pankhurst, 1957, 13).

John Stuart Mill's outburst to Gustave D'Eichthal in 1829 was an indication of the appeal of that remarkable French thinker St. Simon, who had 'cast upon the waters of discussion more interesting and instructive ideas than anyone since Rousseau' (*Ibid.* 123).

Those interesting ideas were boundlessly optimistic. Industry to St. Simon was to be Christianised to 'ameliorate the condition of the poor far more than any of the measures hitherto taken by temporary or spiritual powers'. His disciples came to England in 1831. Here they called upon William Johnson Fox (the Oldham nonconformist minister who twenty years later was to introduce an education bill for rate and state aided education), Anna Wheeler (the apostle of co-operation) and that indefatigable school founder Lady Noel Byron. Their message led Mill to describe them as 'the only association of public writers existing in the world who systematically stir up from the foundation all the great social questions, even those which have been settled long ago' (Pankhurst, 1957, 73).

For their sanguine hopes about the future—which would include a United States of Europe—had a strong educational component. To prepare children for 'the golden age of the human race' the St.-Simonians looked to the spread of Pestalozzianism. 'Our lives' declared two other St.-Simonian publicists in Britain, 'have been directed to the science of education. We have acquired at the institutions of Pestalozzi, Fellenberg, Père Girard, the necessary experience for this task' (*Ibid.* 129). Their belief in the efficacy of the non-didactic community-centred methods of these three Swiss pioneers was also shared by many others for whom the technocratic, pan-European visions of St.-Simon had no appeal. Certainly in the heady exchanges of those times, the spread of Pestalozzianism owed much to the sedulous propaganda of the St.-Simonian school, and some of the English who flirted with it—like Lady Noel Byron.

St.-Simonian influence extends down the century. One disciple, Michel Chevalier, was to sign a memorable commercial treaty with England in 1860. Another, Arles Dufour, was described by Lyon Playfair as having 'great influence on the educational progress of his time' (Wemyss Reid, 1899, 163).

The nineteenth century Edict of Nantes: the loi Falloux

But after the communist interlude in the third French Revolution of 1848 many French moderates changed their minds. 'Let us run and throw ourselves at the feet of the bishops,' said Victor Cousin, 'they alone are able to save us today' (Collins, 1923, 270–1). So too, Thiers regarded 'religion and its ministers as the auxiliaries, the saviours, perhaps, of the social order, which is threatened ... I regard liberty of instruction as useful, even necessary in the face of a system of obligatory demagogic instruction'.

Put by the 1848 Revolution in the same position of having to capture the co-operation of the Catholic Church, Louis Napoleon invited the devouted Catholic Falloux to the ministry of worship and education. Falloux refused to accept unless Napolean allowed him to prepare a bill for 'educational liberty'. Supported by many of the bourgeoisie, he was able to abolish the monopoly of the *université* and allow *écoles libres*, run by an individual or a church, to exist by the side of their schools. Nevertheless the Catholics opposed it, and it was only when the church primary and secondary schools became viable challengers of the state that their hostility abated, and the Abbé Lacordaire could hail it as 'The Edict of Nantes of the nineteenth century'. It was certainly divisive if not decisive.

Christianising socialism

Having seen in Paris, on a return visit in 1848, the 'menace' of socialism, John M. Ludlow, a former pupil of the *Collège Bourbon*, who had come to practise conveyancing in England, wrote to his friend the chaplain of Lincoln's Inn urging that unless such a force was christianised it would shake society to its foundations. This view had also been held by Thomas Arnold. Arnold was dead, but his disciple, Thomas Hughes, then a regular attender at Lincoln's Inn Chapel, had caught enough of his message to understand when it was explained to him by Ludlow, Maurice and another Anglican clergyman, Charles Kingsley.

Together they launched a weekly—*Politics for the People*—which lasted for two months. For it Ludlow wrote thirty-eight articles, stressing the concept of association, which he had seen at work in France among the *Société des amis des pauvres*. Other old Rugbeians also joined and the Christian Socialist Movement was under way.

Further French inspiration was forthcoming in the person of A. L. Jules le Chevalier (whom they knew as St. André), an apostle of the 'associative spirit'. With his help was formed the Society for Promoting Working Men's Associations. This worked for producer co-operatives and a Central Co-operative Agency as an outlet for the products of the producers' societies and an inlet for consumers' societies. This ideal of producer co-operation was to haunt the Christian Socialist Movement for the rest of the century.

One educational by-product of the movement developed from a school for working men established in Little Ormond Yard. Thanks to an earlier venture at Sheffield, the Christian Socialists established a Working Men's College at 31 Red Lion Square in connection with the metropolitan associations.

'Timely preparation': M. Arnold's insurance against Americanisation

'Christianising' workers was only a partial approach to the real problem. As Matthew Arnold put it in 1861:

> almost everyone believes in the growth of democracy, almost everyone talks of it, almost everyone laments it; but the last thing people can be brought to do is to make timely preparation for it (Super, 1962, ii, 19).

That 'timely preparation' was, for Arnold, the strengthening of the power of the State. Only the State, he argued, could 'help us to prevent the English people from becoming, with the growth of democracy *Americanised*' (Super, 1962, ii, 16). Americanisation, in his sense, meant 'low ideals and want of culture' (*Ibid*. 25). By ensuring that the middle classes were educated, the state could prevent them 'exaggerating their spirit of individualism' (*Ibid*. 25). That is why he rejoiced in the opportunity to become an assistant commissioner for the Newcastle Commission, appointed on 30 June 1858 'to consider and report what measures, if any, are required for the Extension of sound and cheap elementary instruction to all classes of the people'. Arriving in Paris 15 March 1859 he finally returned to England (after visiting other countries) on 26 August. The most recent editor of his findings has observed that:

> there can be little doubt that the intimate knowledge he gained of France and the personal acquaintance with her statesmen and literary men were of the first im-

portance to the development of his career as a writer (Super, 1962, ii, 329).

His report, published in the fourth volume of the New-castle Commission was also published separately as a book, *The Popular Education of France with Notices of that of Holland and Switzerland* (1861). It carried a direct message to his fellow countrymen that the time had arrived . . .

> when it is becoming impossible for the aristocracy of England to conduct and wield the English nation any longer (p. 6) . . . Democracy is trying to *affirm its own essence*; to live, to enjoy, to possess the world, as aristocracy has tried, and successfully tried before it . . . (p. 7).
>
> The power of France in Europe is at this day mainly owing to the completeness with which she has organised democratic institutions . . . (p. 10).
>
> 'I know,' he continued, 'what a chorus of objectors will be ready. One will say : Rather repair and restore the influence of aristocracy. Another will say : It is not a bad thing, but a good thing, that the English people should be Americanised. But the most formidable and the most widely entertained objection, by far, will be that which founds itself upon the present actual state of things in another country; which says : Look at France. There you have a signal example of the alliance of democracy with a powerful State-action, and see how it works' (p. 16).

The appointment of another Royal commission under Lord Clarendon on 18 July 1861 to enquire into the condition of the nine most distinguished public schools led Arnold to draw on his French experience and write *A French Eton*. This posed the fundamental question why could not the English organise schools where the children of the middle and professional classes could obtain :

> . . . an education of as good quality, with as good guarantees, social character, and advantages for a

future career in the world, as the education which French children of the corresponding class can obtain from institutions like that of Toulouse or Sorèze.

In this powerful appeal to the middle classes to favour state action to establish a system of public instruction, Arnold warned that the clergy were moving into vacuum now and that unless the middle class moved

it would not be easy hereafter, in secondary instruction, to settle the religious difficulty equitably, if the establishment of that instruction shall have been effected by public bodies in which clerical influence predominates (Super, 1962, ii, 324).

As he told his mother on 11 February 1864:

I am convinced that nothing can be done to raise this [the working] class except through the agency of a transformed middle class; for, till the middle class is transformed, the aristocratic class, which will do nothing effectively, will rule.

Arnold's advocacy of positive state action was quickly challenged. In the *Pall Mall Gazette*, a newspaper founded in February 1865, as well as in the older *Times*, articles were carried exposing his ideas, though the *Pall Mall Gazette*, by allowing him to reply on the following day (20 December 1865), served his purpose more closely.

When a third royal commission was set up on 29 July 1864 (largely owing to Arnold's advocacy) to examine the ways in which secondary education could be made more generally available in England, Arnold suggested that someone should be sent to report on what state action had accomplished on the continent. To his delight that someone was himself.

So on 9 April he was in Paris again. And again his report, drafted with much labour, was also published as a book, this time by Macmillans in 1868. This was Volume VI of the Report of the Schools Inquiry Commission: *Schools and Universities on the Continent* (1868). It gave so favourable a review of French education that the *Pall Mall Gazette* (24 March 1868) wrote:

> We should not be surprised, if some good and far-seeing despot were to find himself endowed with absolute power in this country, to see him placing Mr. Arnold in such a position as that of M. Duruy in France, and banishing Mr. Robert Lowe to Cayenne.

7

The triple scarecrow: secularism, sociologism and scientism

Jean Macé and the French National Education League

In 1866 Jean Macé, a popular science writer and teacher, founded the French Educational League. This conducted a nation-wide campaign for libraries and later for free, secular and compulsory education. Branches formed in large towns. A petition was organised and powerful politicians recruited.

Singularly enough the director of a foreign merchanting house, who knew France well, happened to be Mayor of Birmingham at this very time, and was confronted with some serious anti-popery riots in the town. As a result, he convened some conferences on the religious question. From these developed an organisation with exactly the same structure and programme as Macé's.

But whereas the Birmingham National Education League was able to take action to press its programme on the Government, Macé's had virtually to hold its hand because of the France-Prussian War. But when the war was over, it got going again, this time in the shape of a popular movement which was known as 'The Commission of the National Halfpenny Movement Against Ignorance'.

Confronted by a 150-volume petition from Macé's League on one side and Monsignor Doupanloup, spokesman of the Catholic majority, on the other, the National Assembly shelved the question.

Not until the positivist Jules Ferry took over, first the Ministry of Public Instruction, then the premiership, did its case prosper. Secular normal schools were instituted in every department to train teachers and higher grade elementary normal schools for those who were to train the teachers. Two years later, in 1881, education was made free. Priests and members of religious orders were forbidden to teach or keep schools without a state certificate. Compulsory attendance at schools independent of church and sect was decreed in 1882. The Jesuits were expelled and their schools closed.

Ferry also made provision for the secondary education of girls, and encouraged the teaching of science.

Cardinal Manning's fears and actions

Such events alarmed English observers. Cardinal Manning, the spokesman for the Catholic Schools in England, told his prime minister that he believed that the siege of Paris was 'traceable in chief to a godless education' . . . 'The worst disaster that could befall us would be an "Imperial Education". It must be godless.' He was referring to the commune, set up in Paris after the French defeat in 1870 (McClelland, 1962, 75).

His misgivings, intensified by the savage treatment of the Archbishop of Paris, governed his arguments against England adopting a secular system of board schools in 1870. Though he had the satisfaction of being told by Gladstone that 'you and the government are on the same lines with respect to this important matter' (Purcell, 1896, ii, 493), his efforts to prevent a secular French-type education being imposed on England progressively intensified.

Fearing that the contagion of continental free thought and agnosticism would spread from Oxford and Cambridge to the Catholic laity, and already critical of their unrepresentative character, Cardinal Manning, like Newman, was anxious to emulate the French Catholics, who had set up their own universities in France. Newman, having left Dublin (see p. 47) was in favour of a Roman Catholic college or house at Oxford, but Manning wanted to found a proper Roman Catholic University College.

As a site he favoured South Kensington because of the examinations and cultural faculties already provided by the University of London. So his college opened there in October 1874 with professors of Biology, Chemistry and Modern History as well as Hebrew and Classics, reflecting Manning's own vivid involvement in contemporary affairs. The principal, Monsignor Capel, had experience of the new French higher education, having spent eight years as a lecturer at Pau in the South of France. His appointment was, perhaps, the biggest reason for the college's collapse, though the hostility of the Jesuits, the lukewarm attitude of the bishops and Newman's aloofness weakened it from the outset. So in 1878 it was amalgamated with St. Charles's College, Kensington, as an 'advanced department'.

When Jules Ferry began to establish free compulsory education and followed up by abolishing religious instruction altogether in French state schools, Manning was even more alarmed. He founded the Voluntary Schools Association to monitor the Birmingham radicals and their anticlerical leader Chamberlain and work for the re-opening of the 1870 settlement through a Royal Commission. Manning wanted rate aid for Roman Catholic schools and used the 'depraving' effects of French secularism as a stalking horse.

Even Matthew Arnold changed his mind and in 1882 was deploring the modern French schoolboy, 'Voltairian and emancipated . . . making it his pastime to play tricks on his chaplain, to mock and flout him and his teaching' (Campos, 1965, 41). Not only the growing secularism, but the republicanism of France repelled him and he began to compare its condition to the fall of Greece, Rome and Italy.

When Chamberlain raised the cry of 'free education' in the 1885 election, Manning ordered his flock, before voting, to assess their parliamentary candidates' attitude to the programme of the Voluntary Schools Association. He was successful. The Liberals were defeated. 'What we need,' he told Bishop Vaughan of Salford after the election, 'is a permanent settlement and protection against Chamberlain and Jules Ferry' (McClelland, 1962, 85). He certainly got it. His much desired Royal Commission was appointed, with himself as a very active member. So active indeed that he swayed a majority to recommend, in 1888, that voluntary schools should be helped from the rates. And this, too, was also secured by the 1902 Act.

The Ferry system—or *la morale laïque*—became a shuttlecock in the war of attrition between the sects. Englishmen were told by their favourite American journalist (until he was compromised in a breach of promise case in 1891) that 'nothing can be more certain than that the educational legislation of France since 1882 has been aimed steadily and directly at the abolition, not of Christianity alone, but of all religion' (Hurlbut, 1890, 35). French provisions for systematic moral instruction with a non-theological content were thought by some Englishmen to be so adequate, that the Moral Instruction League was formed in 1897 under Harrold Johnson to promote similar systematic non-theological moral education in British schools. But the Church of England objected, citing the increase of suicides and divorces (Rees, 1908, 307–8). So did the Roman Catholics, who attributed the assassination of the French and American presidents to the expulsion of God from their schools (Sacks, 1961, 120–2). Believers in the Ferry system retorted that in any case the blame should be laid at the doors of the Roman Catholic Church which had controlled the schools for so long. One Congregationalist M.P. went so far as to accuse the Roman Catholics in France of helping to produce the autocrat Boulanger and of aggravating the hatreds released in the Dreyfus affair.

Sociologism: Émile Durkheim, Le Play and Sir Patrick Geddes

Since the time of Comte, who first coined the word sociology in 1835 to describe the 'social physics' needed in the scientific industrial age, there had developed an increasingly secular morality. After the defeat of 1870, positivists turned to education as a means of ensuring moral unity and social conformity. Émile Durkheim, appointed at the University of Bordeaux in 1887, gave the first proper sociology course in a French university, lecturing in education as well. For to him education was 'the methodical socialisation of the young'. The creation of the necessary physical, intellectual and moral states demanded by society and the social milieu for which the individual was intended, was, to Durkheim, the problem of education. He saw the difficulties of those occluded or rejected from the societal embrace as leading to suicide (Albert, 1961, 59).

Sociology indeed became the new cult of France. Thanks to the *Année Sociologique* founded by Durkheim in 1889, and to the work of René Worms and Gabriel Tarde, France became a centre of such interest that an American, writing from the Paris Exposition in 1900, observed 'of all the countries in the world that are contributing to the sociological movement England displayed least activity, France most' (Ward, 1901).

There was a Scotsman, however, of whom this could not be said: Patrick Geddes. Greatly influenced by his attendance at the *Société internationale des études practiques de l'économie sociale* in 1878, he absorbed the teaching of its great founder Frederic Le Play. To him it was essential '*To see the thing as it is*' and '*to make the thing as it should be*'. One was the 'morality of truth', the other the 'morality of action' and Paris was to him 'the hardest working of all great cities' (Mairet, 1957, 26). Twenty-two years later he was to organise an international school at the Paris Exhibition of 1900 in conjunction with the brothers Elisé and Elie Réclus.

This school was the forerunner of further organisations in England—a British National Institute for Geographers and the Sociological Society. The first was still-born, the second became the 'church', to spread, through the *Sociological Review*, Geddes' ideas on civics interpreted through the Environment, the Function and the Organism.

Geddes' imaginative approach to town planning commended itself to his assistants and pupils. Some of them, like A. J. Herbertson, became geographers. Others like Lewis Mumford, who helped him with his *Sociological Review*, popularised his terms for the successive age of culture: 'paleotechnic', 'neo-technic' and 'eotechnic'. Others like 'megalopolis' and 'conurbation' have passed into common use. To emancipate his countrymen 'from Pre-Germanic universities like Oxford and Sub-Germanic ones like Cambridge, so that we may learn in the Post-Germanic school of French thought' (Mairet, 1957, 126) he purposed to revive the Scots College in Paris, but switched it to Montpellier.

This experiment in the *Cité Universitaire* of tomorrow exercised a profound influence on the town planning movement.

The industrial exhibitions and the spirit of emulation

The Centenary Exhibition of French art and industry held on the *Champs de Mars* and in the Trocadéro gardens in 1889, with the tower designed by Alexander Gustave Eiffel and the great *Galerie des Machines*, symbolised not only the recovery of France from the defeat of 1870, but recalled the effect of previous French exhibitions in England.

It was a reminder, if any were needed, that these great ecumenical councils of technology dated from Revolutionary times. The original one, mounted in Paris in 1791, had attracted a mere 110 exhibitors, but over the next fifty-three years eight subsequent exhibitions attracted 220, 540, 1,422, 1,662, 1,642, 2,447, 3,381, and 3,960 exhibitors respectively, till by 1848 there were 4,532.

The first English attempts were made by G. J. W. Agar-Ellis at King's Mews, now the site of the National Gallery. He found, however, that the Brigade of Guards were using it, so subsequent exhibitions were abandoned. 'Sacrificed' as Birkbeck complained, 'to Lord Hill and the drummers of the Guards' (Kelly, 1957, 181).

Not until the young English architect, Matthew Digby Wyatt was sent over by the Royal Society of Arts to report on the 1848 Paris Exhibition was another attempt made to mount another exhibition in London (Hitchcock, 1952, 16). Wyatt's report to the Royal Society of Arts (formed as an exhibition-staging body), led to the appointment of a Royal Commission to sponsor the project. Indeed, of the 245 designs submitted for an exhibition, one of the two selected for 'special mention' was French: a modified scheme for the Paris markets designed by Hector Horeau. The other was designed by the builder of the Lime Street railway station (Richard Turner). Neither were chosen. Instead the Duke of Devonshire's head gardener built a great prefabricated greenhouse in Hyde Park to house the exhibition: the Crystal Palace.

From the profits of this exhibition—some £186,000—and a special Parliamentary grant—some £150,000—were built the first buildings of the complex that is now the Imperial College of Science and Technology, as well as the first offices for new government departments of Science and Art. As a result of another exhibition four years later at Paris (on which Wyatt also reported) these departments were combined to become the distributors of the first government grants for science teaching in England.

Such teaching received a further shot in the arm when the University of London not only instituted science degrees in 1858 but allowed all its degrees (with the exception of those in medicine) to be taken by all comers.

France, quoted by some of the advocates of the above change, appeared so formidable to Englishmen in 1859 that the Poet-Laureate urged his fellow countrymen to

Let your reforms for a moment go
Look to your butts and take your arms,
Better a rotten borough or so
Than a rotten fleet and a city in flames.

Rifle corps were started. P.T. was organised in the schools. A gymnasium—the first in any public school—was built by Uppingham. But the scare passed. In 1860 a commercial treaty was signed between the two countries and in 1861 Arnold returned with the suggestion that the University of London should have branches in at least ten different parts of England organised by a French-type Minister of Education, advised by a High Council that would regulate studies and adjust school and university examinations: a striking anticipation of our present Schools Council.

Further moves towards a French pattern of technical and scientific training were suggested as a result of the poor showing of British exhibits in the 1867 Paris Exhibition. The great administrator, Edwin Chadwick, cited the *École Centrale des Arts et Métiers* as worthy of emulation. Even the Napoleonic university found a strong advocate in a former associate of the Prince Consort—the marine engineer, John Scott Russell, who in 1869 advocated a French-style national technological university federated with fifteen local colleges. A committee was set up at 4 Storey's Gate, St. James's Park which tried to interest the government in his proposal.

This, like other proposals, did not fall on deaf ears. Local initiative started colleges in the great northern and midland industrial towns and Bristol. These, however,

67

received no state aid, apart from *ad hoc* grants for science students, till 1887.

French provincial universities and their English counterparts

From 1890 too, French universities were reconstituted. In that year six provincial ones were christened at Lille, Lyons, Bordeaux, Montpellier, Nancy and Toulouse. Perhaps recreated would be a better term, as universities had existed in these towns since 1562, 1888, 1411, 1180, 1572 and 1220 respectively. Six years later eight more were chartered: Aix-Marseilles (1409), Besançon (1422), Caen (1431), Clermont-Ferrand (1810), Dijon (1722), Grenoble (1339), Poitiers (1432) and Rennes (1461). These fourteen replaced the local but exclusive boards of the Imperial University by General Councils of the Faculties (*Conseils de l'Université*). So each university acquired a legal status and financial autonomy of its own and though its teachers were paid by the state and its degrees were co-ordinated by the state, each could enjoy their own income as they were empowered to receive gifts. Teachers were now recruited by co-option with central approval.

Having no 'universities', as the English understood them, from 1808 to 1896, but boards of faculties in the seventeen academies, France now had fourteen provincial universities plus a rebuilt and revitalised Sorbonne. Little wonder then that the architect of these reforms, Louis Liard, (who also wrote a standard history of higher education in France) was cited freely in the debates on the 1898 Bill for inducing London University to cultivate its regional resources. The passage of the London University Act was followed by a rise to local autonomy of the provincial universities which soon afterwards successfully supplicated for charters: Birmingham in 1900, Manchester, Liverpool and Leeds in 1903, Sheffield in 1905 and Bristol in 1909.

The replacement of the Napoleonic University by

fifteen independent universities was described in 1903 by the President of the British Association for the Advancement of Science as part of a 'strenuous effort' in securing 'a higher quality and greater quantity of brain power': the University of Paris being with its 13,000 students 'truly marvellous' (Lockyer, 1903, 21).

English rationalist Francophiles

'It is an education itself to have heard such men converse or lecture,' ruminated Frederic Harrison (1911, ii, 65), looking back at his friendship with Jules Ferry, Gambetta, Thiers and numerous other Frenchmen. For Harrison was the leading apostle in England of the Positivists. He was once told by Auguste Comte that 'without due training in the physical sciences it was idle to attempt to solve the ultimate problems' (Harrison, 1911, ii, 253). So Harrison continued his scientific education whilst practising as a lawyer in London.

Harrison's Oxford tutor, Richard Congreve founded the Positivist Society in 1867. This embraced a number of those who were active middle class workers on behalf of the Trade Unions, then beginning their fight for recognition as negotiating bodies. Positivists were therefore little better than republicans to Englishmen. Matthew Arnold particularly made fun of Frederic Harrison in his *Culture and Anarchy* (1867). But Harrison won through, establishing in Newton Hall, London, a School, Club and Chapel, a people's school on the lines of a Mechanics' Institute, offering free lectures of a popular kind, and using it as a basis of Positivist propaganda (Simon, 1963, 202–237).

Another sympathetic receptor of French sociology (especially of Alfred Fouillée) was the ex-rector of St. Bernadine's College, Buckingham, Joseph McCabe. A doughty rationalist (the adjective might well be doubting), he withdrew from the Church of Rome in 1896 to devote himself to the debates on the 1902 Act, showing that the numbers of delinquents in French reformatories had lowered rather than increased. He was one of the pillars of *The Free Thinker*, a journal of the National Secular Society. An even more reputable group, embracing labour leaders like Ramsay McDonald, Arthur Henderson, Philip Snowden and Thomas Burt; novelists and writers like Havelock Ellis and H. G. Wells, together with Anglican and Nonconformist ministers like the Rt. Rev. Murchinson, the Rev. Steward D. Headlam and the Rev. R. J. Campbell, was formed on 4 February 1907. This was the Secular Education League, designed to exclude the teaching of religion in state-supported elementary schools in school hours or at public expense.

But in spite of the revelations of damage done in the school system by the religious disputes, they had a hard press.

Their efforts were forwarded by a group of powerful Francophile thinkers with access to the public ear: John Morley (biographer of Voltaire, Rousseau and the Encyclopaedists), Augustine Birrell (who introduced the abortive 1906 Education Bill) and J. B. Bury, professor of modern history at Cambridge from 1912 to 1927—a historian who emphasised the unity and continuity of Europe in, amongst other works, his *History of Freedom of Thought* (1964) and his *Idea of Progress* (1920). With them should be numbered J. M. Robertson, of whom the late Harold Laski said: 'Few people since the great French encyclopaedist Bayle have had so wide a range of significant knowledge' (*D.N.B.*, 1949, 736).

8

L'humanisme totale

Budin, Binet and Braille

The whole cost of the war indemnity paid by France to
Germany in 1870 was, in T. H. Huxley's opinion, more
than covered by the discoveries of Pasteur. For Pasteur's
discovery that fermentation in milk is a kind of putre-
faction caused by air-borne micro-organisms opened up a
new chapter in public health. This was recognised in
England as early as 1865 by Joseph (later Lord) Lister
who applied Pasteur's principle in surgery by insisting
on sterilisation of the wound, the instruments, and the
surgeon's hands. Antiseptic and aseptic techniques which
followed from this opened new doors in medicine. One
of Pasteur's disciples first conceived child welfare as an
independent study and gave it a name: *puériculture*.
This was Émile Duclaux who began to lecture on social
hygiene at the *École des Hautes Études Sociales* in 1902.
Other disciples, like Dr. Budin, obstetrician at *La
Charité* hospital in Paris organised, towards the end of
the nineteenth century, a successful campaign against
infantile mortality by advocating the use of pasteurised
milk for infants who could not be breast fed. His *'Gouttes
de lait'* saved thousands of children yearly from gastric
enteritis. His work was endorsed in England by the Dean

of the Faculty of Medicine at Edinburgh, Sir Alexander Simpson, himself an old student at Montpellier. Budin's campaign for child welfare clinics resulted in 494 being established in France by 1907: the year he died.

The first English 'milk stations' were opened at St. Helens in 1899 where suitably sterilised modified milk was made available on the advice of a doctor. By 1901 Infant Welfare Centres, with sterilised milk available, were opened in Liverpool and the practice spread through the country by the Maternity and Child Welfare Act of 1918. At the same time his fellow doctor, Alfred Binet, attracted the attention of F. Buisson, who in 1900 founded the *Societé libre pour l'etude de la psychologie de l'enfant*. Binet's *L'étude experimentale d'intelligence* (1903)—itself the record of an experimental study on two girls of contrasting types—led Buisson to ask him to devise a diagnostic instrument for measuring mental defects. By 1905 he produced the first scale for the measurement of intelligence from tests on hundreds of children and extended this to measuring normal children.

With his collaborator, Dr. Simon, he tested most of the children in Parisian primary schools and, as a result, special classes for backward children were established. In one such school he opened an educational centre with apparatus and material for discussions with teachers. These fortnightly sessions strengthened *La Societé Libre de l'étude psychologique de l'enfant* whose *Bulletin* stirred much interest in England. Indeed Binet's book *Les idées modernes sur les enfants* (1907) virtually outlined new fields for research, and inspired, amongst others, Professor J. A. Green of Sheffield to interest himself in such tests.

Nor, in this inadequate indication of the influence of French techniques on English social medicine, should we forget the work of Dr. T. R. Armitage, who discerned that the system of reading by raised dots as pioneered by M. Braille at the *Institution nationale des jeunes Aveugles* offered a way out of the conflicting welter of 'systems' offered to the blind in the 1860s. So out of his own pocket he established the British and Foreign Blind Association (now the National Institute for the Blind) to issue books, magazines and music in Braille. Thanks to the accession of the publisher, Sir C. Arthur Pearson, to its council, the Association was able to raise money for new buildings in Great Portland Street, and establish Braille as the standard technique of reading for the blind.

Mandarinism in British science

The mandarinate of English, as opposed to French, science at this time is perhaps epitomised by the fact that at the first meeting of the International Association of Academies held in Paris in 1900, Britain was represented only by the Royal Society. This was doubly unfortunate in that both before and after the meeting the Royal Society decisively refused either to widen its own scope or to initiate the establishment of an academy of suitable representatives from such fields of study.

Through such an academy, 'somewhat resembling the famous *Académie Française* had been advocated for at least thirty years (*Macmillan's Magazine* flirted with the idea in March 1864). It took this international conference in Paris to activate a group to consider how best to satisfy the requirements of the International Association of Academies. Meeting at the British Museum on 28 June 1901, they decided six months later to found the British Academy. But, even then, this was confined to 'the Promotion of Historical Philosophical and Philological Studies', and received a charter as such on 8 August 1902.

Even in the field of pure science the Royal Society was criticised as an exclusive club.

Complaining that election to the Royal Society was 'an invitation to repose rather than as incentive to work' Professor J. Y. Buchanan, F.R.S., the wealthy and melancholy geographer, explorer and traveller was moved to write to *Nature* in 1904.

How different is the state of things which we observe in the parallel society in France, the Academy of Sciences. Its constitution is thoroughly democratic, and all its proceedings are inspired by enlightened self-respect. But we need only contemplate the work which it puts through in the year and compare it with what is turned out by the Royal Society to see that there is something for us to learn by its study.

First and foremost the academy meets fifty-two times in the year, namely, on every Monday, with the exception of Easter Monday and Whit Monday, and then it meets on the following Tuesdays. By the time-table of the current year the Royal Society is to meet twenty times.

Buchanan complained about the habit of referring papers by Fellows and the delay in publication whereas in the French Academies:

The communication, reading, and publication of a paper presented to the academy is therefore an affair of the inside of a week, and it is a certainty. This promptitude in the putting through of work is due to the fundamental fact that when a man is elected a member of the academy he enters at once into the full enjoyment of all its privileges, and one of the chief of these is the complete confidence of all his fellow-members (1904, 292).

The equally brilliant and unconventional physicist Oliver Heaviside, agreed:

What Mr. J. Y. Buchanan says about the French Academy is to me much more wonderful than the revelations of radium. It appears that there is a happy land close by where a scientific man of recognised standing can indulge in the luxury of original research, and then send in an account of his work, *not* to have it rejected by the opinion of, say, a couple of fellow-men, but actually to have it published as a right! This seems impossible. It is the encouragement of original research. Perhaps it is hopeless to expect such freedom in this stick-in-the-mud country, which is so much in love with tradition and antiquated forms. Without any desire to be 'contumelious', I would say that our Royal Society reminds me of the House of Lords in many respects (1904, 317).

French pacemakers in electrical engineering

Heaviside's generous opinion of the organisation of French science had some justification. For in his own fields, mathematical physics and electricity, the French scientists had made massive advances. Lesage's production of the first static electricity telegraph in 1774, Volta's discovery of the Voltaic pile in 1800, Pixii's first rotating dynamo in 1832, Pouillet's large galvanometer of 1837 : all contributed to the illumination of the Paris Opera House by hand-operated arc lamps by 1844.

Whilst other nations were acquiring the technical skill, the French first lightened darkness by electricity. From the installation in 1862 of a French arc lamp in Dungeness lighthouse, similar systems were installed by the *Compagnie de l'Alliance* whose 'Alliance' machines captured the imagination. Even more successful was another French company, *La Société Générale d'Électricité* which devised the first arc lamp to be used on a large scale for illuminating public places. From the Breguet factory in Paris came the Jablochkoff candle subsequently (1877) patented in Britain, powered by a Breguet alternator devised by Gramme.

Gramme's dynamo was the great success of the Paris Exposition of 1878, illuminating half a mile of the L'Avenue and Place de l'Opéra. Gramme's co-operation with the *Société Générale d'Électricité* of Paris had already lit the Gare du Nord in 1875 and the Grands Magasins du Louvre in 1877. Such developments, as *The Electrician* pointed out on 20 July 1878, were still far in advance of what had been achieved in London, where Gramme had successfully lit the House of Commons in 1873. The Old Gaiety Theatre followed, then Billingsgate

Fish Market. The former was the first public building in London to install electric lighting, the latter the first example of public enterprise in electric lighting. Then came the illumination of the Embankment by agreement between the old Metropolitan Board of Works and the *Société Générale d'Électricité* of Paris. Similar agreements provided light for Holborn Viaduct and the Mansion House.

The establishment of *The Electrician* in 1878 as a repository for every phase of progress (it carried a number of Heaviside's research papers), was but one indication of the quickening interest in this new development. Another was the establishment in the following year, of the City and Guilds of London Institute at Finsbury where two electrical engineers, W. E. Ayrton and John Perry, were appointed to chairs and threw themselves into the task of providing adequate facilities for the training of electrical engineers. Ayrton's first wife had practised medicine, incidentally, in Algiers and Montpellier. Ayrton also undertook in 1878 the editorship of the *Journal* of the already thriving Institution of Telegraph Engineers. This body took cognisance of developments and changed their title in 1889 to become the Institution of Electrical Engineers. Ayrton undertook the editing of its *Journal*.

The subsequent migration of the City and Guilds to Exhibition Road in 1884 was symbolic, for the centralising of technical schools on that site was itself yet another attempt to provide a centre of special excellence in technological education, being a component part of the Imperial College of Science and Technology.

French technology: the Corbusier 'modulor'

For France was breaking other technological barriers. Cultivation of talent was now bearing fruit. The daguerrotype had taken form in the hands of an opera-scene painter, L. J. M. Daguerre, who founded the Diorama in Paris in 1822, and with the help of the physicist J. N.

Niepce had produced permanent pictures on metal and glass plates by the action of sunlight. Another physicist C. F. A. Niepce de Saint-Victor was one of the first to produce sheet engravings by photographic means. Their contemporary in England, W. H. F. Talbot, patented his 'instantaneous photograph' in 1851. Characteristically, Daguerre's patents were bought by the French Government, and later pioneers went on to devise colour photography (Cros, Ducros de Hauron and Gabriel Lippman). So did two chemists, Louis Jean and Auguste Lumière, who manufactured photographic materials and invented an early motion picture camera in 1893.

In the air Louis Mouillard's remarkable *L'Empire de l'Air* (1881) was widely read and inspired Octave Chanute and the Wright brothers (Davy, 1948, 99). In the field of transport, engineering skill had devised cooling systems, carburretors, cam-shafts (Forest), pneumatic tyres (Michelin) and the differential (Oennicker), so that by 1909 there were 205 automobile factories in France—more than in Britain (62), the United States (111), Austria (4) and Belgium (18) combined.

Air races elicited not only the achievements of Santos-Dumont, who built the first airship station at Neuilly in 1903, but Blériot's achievement in flying the first heavier than air machine across the channel six years later.

Even the house was becoming a machine in the imagination of the French, and the *École des Beaux Arts* had become the design centre for Europe. Henri Labrouste built the *Bibliothèque St.-Geneviève* and the *Bibliothèque Nationale*, and by exploiting the internal iron column frame with heavy masonry exteriors, set the trend. Even more so did Viollet-le-Duc, who from his appointment to the school in 1863 demanded rationality of structure. His *Entretiens sur l'Architecture* (1863–72) stressed the importance of function and material as the determinants of form. So too Frank Lloyd Wright, the American pioneer of new styles, was told by his father to read Viollet-le-Duc's writings as offering all the basic education needed. This doctrine of 'functionalism' influenced architects not trained in Paris, like Le Corbusier, who was born in 1887, eight years after Viollet-le-Duc died.

Le Corbusier's houses were 'machines for living in'; his 'change-over towns' were metropoli with diverse functions. He devised 'norms' for building. His was the modulor, based on the initial dimensions of an upright six foot man with his hand raised (7 ft 5 ins or 225 cm). Little wonder that his disciples regarded architecture as part of 'l'humanisme totale'.

L'École Normale and the French Left

But of all the nurseries of l'humanisme totale, the most celebrated was in the Rue d'Ulm in Paris: the *École Normale Supérieure*. This from the year 1898 when the epic 'Manifesto of the Intellectuals' was issued at the height of the Dreyfus affair, has been most closely identified as a nursery of 'intellectuals'. This class, more highly regarded in France than anywhere else in the world (Caute, 1964, 11), now veered definitely, some say 'naturally', (Lüthy, 1960, 444) to the Left. Intellectual and *normalien* became interchangeable terms. This institution produced the leaders which made France unique in Western Europe for having, not only a communist party with a continuous existence since 1920, but in having seriously to discuss its programme, since many of the best French scientists and teachers of the thirties and forties were party members (Caute, 1964, 261–31). They also made available much information about the new Soviet belief in education as a solvent of social class and a spur to economic achievement.

9

Franco-British technical co-operation

The Entente and after

The obvious desire of French statesmen to obtain the
support of British sea power, the mutual need of both
countries to reach an understanding over Africa, and the
increasing threat of German technical advance led, from
1902 onwards, to a series of visits and talks between
ambassadors and heads of state. These culminated two
years later in the signature of the Anglo-French conventions of 8 April 1904.

To give 'practical shape to the entente' a Franco-British
Exhibition was organised on an 140-acre site in Shepherd's
Bush in 1908. In this, both countries professed to 'join
hands in happy union for the purpose of setting before
the world their combined resources'. These combined
resources included 'Anglo-Saxon energy blended with
savoir faire, empiricism adorned by method, solidity
adorned by grace to provide a combination which em-
braces the highest achievement of the human race'.

Certainly the experience of working together stood the
two countries in good stead six years later as French
scientists had to play a major role in the mutual war
against Germany. They met the threat of gas warfare by
improvising the first gas mask (Andre Mayer and Paul

Lebeau). They devised sonar to detect German submarines (Langevin, Pierre and Jacques Curie), and sound location to detect German batteries (Nordman and Esclangon). They headed the technical services of the Allies (Moureu, Grignard, Urbain and Job). Even their Minister of War and Premier in 1917 was a mathematician, Paul Painlevé, who, with Perrin, Lapicque and Cotton was a mainspring of the Service des Inventions.

This incipient Anglo-French technocracy of the First World War was to develop not in, but after, the Second World War.

The 1940 proposal for union and the Monnet plan

Seven days after he had arrived in London in 1940 to rally British help for the French armies in headlong retreat before the Germans, General de Gaulle was presented with a shattering proposal: nothing less than the complete merger of Britain and France into a single state with one cabinet, one united war effort, one common citizenship. The proposal certainly justified the description of being 'the most drastic scheme for supranational integration that anyone has ever presented, on a government level, before or since' (Beloff 1963, 43). Approved by the British Cabinet, it was rejected by the French, who promptly sued for a separate peace with Germany.

The draftsman of this plan was M. Monnet, then chairman of the Anglo-French Supply Mission. Though an old French dream—it went back before Aristide Briand (who had proposed it to the League of Nations in 1931) to St. Simon and the technocrats, to the Abbé de St. Pierre and Leibniz—it was a persistent one, and it has coloured the political scene up to the time of writing. For Monnet never forgot it. Indeed his own experience of schemes for closer integration was considerable. He had helped co-ordinate supplies for the Allied Forces in the First World War, worked for the League of Nations as Deputy Secretary General, served as a member of the British War

Supplies Council in the Second World War and when his country was liberated, headed French purchasing missions to the U.S.A.

Determined to secure that France would not be a perpetual pensioner of the U.S.A. after the war Monnet drew up a plan for modernisation and investment. A *Commissariat du Plan de Modernisation et d'Équipment* was set up with committees of trade unionists, farmers, industrialists, civil servants and acedemics. It became a nursery of planners. Marjolin left to become secretary of O.E.E.C. and later of the European Economic Community; Hirsch succeeded Monnet as Commissioner-General in 1950 and Monnet himself became President of the European Coal and Steel Community in 1950. Hirsch later left the plan to become President of Euratom in 1959, and was succeeded by the polytechnician M.P. Massé who had been Deputy General Manager of *Électricité de France*.

The Schuman plan and Britain's reaction

These European bodies themselves owed much to M. Monnet—especially the European Coal and Steel Community, of which he became President in 1950. The integration of coal and steel production in France, West Germany, Italy, Holland, Belgium and Luxembourg was sponsored by M. Robert Schuman, and the fifty year treaty instituting the High Authority was signed in Paris in April 1951. As the European Coal and Steel Community, this, rather than the European assembly, was the seed-bed of integration.

Mooted in 1953, and agreed to in 1955, the idea of a Common Market or European Economic Community (E.E.C.) took rapid hold. By the Treaty of Rome, 25 March 1957, the six member states agreed to co-ordinate their national economies to raise their mutual standard of living by eliminating mutual customs barriers, accepting each others' professional qualifications, mutualising banks, insurance, unemployment benefits, and integrating transport.

The rise in production, indeed in the rate of rise from 1959, gave grounds for hope that by 1970 it would have doubled that of 1960. Its success, wrote an external observer, 'would have been impossible without the re-vitalisation and strengthening of the French economy, which was in turn stimulated by the existence of the Common Market (Bramsted, 1963, 57).

With its headquarters in Brussels, in the Avenue de la Joyeuse Entrée—the European Economic Community has become a European Civil Service.

Britain, meanwhile, had been flirting with other schemes. 'The first step in the re-creation of the European family must be a partnership between France and Germany. In this way only can France recover the moral leadership of Europe.' The speaker was Winston Churchill, his audience, the University of Zurich, the date 19 September 1946. Churchill's initiation of a United Europe movement was paralleled by Herriot's formation of a 'Conseil Française pour l'Europe unie'.

A Council of European Ministers

Having signed the Treaty of Brussels in March 1948 with France and the three Benelux countries, Britain was expected to go further. Instead, she held back, agreeing only to a Council of European Ministers, not a Consultative Assembly. Nevertheless, both council and assembly were agreed to in May 1949 at which the five powers were joined by another five (Italy, Denmark, Sweden, Norway and Ireland), and later by another six (Greece, Turkey, Iceland, West Germany, Austria (1956) and Cyprus 1961)). The major weakness of this European Council of Ministers was that they represented their respective national assemblies, not the European Assembly, which indeed was not 'consulted' on anything of importance. Yet, for the first time a supra-national perspective was obtained on problems posed by universities and education generally, to say nothing of social security, mobility of labour, agriculture and transport. As an Australian observer commented, 'if today there are regular meetings between ministers of justice or education, this is due to the initiative of the Council' (Bramsted. 1963, 5).

But faced with closer integration of the Schuman Plan, and later of the Common Market, Britain held back, clinging to her Commonwealth ties, and clutching at her special relationships to the United States. Both perhaps sprang from her ingrained nationalism. Even oblique overtures, embodying the alternative proposal that a European Free Trade Area (E.F.T.A.) should be founded, were summarily rejected by the French on 14 November 1958. So Britain spent the following years assembling six other European states to join her in an 'Outer Seven'.

Set up by the Treaty of Stockholm in January 1960, E.F.T.A. set out from its headquarters at Geneva to reduce tariffs between members by stages analogous to those defined by the Common Market. Unlike the Common Market, however, E.F.T.A. had no superstructure for overall planning and control. It was also smaller: apart from Britain's 51 million, the rest (Norway, Sweden, Denmark, Austria, Switzerland and Portugal), numbered 38 million, as opposed to the Common Market's 170 million. Moreover, as a counter-play against the Common Market it was such a failure that within two years Britain was wanting to leave.

So on 10 August 1961 Britain applied for full membership of the Common Market. Negotiations began in November. Her exports to it had been growing (from 14 to 19 per cent), whilst those to the Commonwealth had been declining (from 47 to 42 per cent) from 1950 to 1960 (de la Mahotière, 1962, 81). Indeed by 1961 Britain exported more to Western Europe than to the whole of the Commonwealth put together (Beloff, 1963, 136).

But having promised her E.F.T.A. partners in the pre-

G

vious June not to enter unless all seven had been admitted as full or associate members, the chance of acceptance was poor (Kleimann, 1965, 99).

The conversion to Europe

A quasi-religious belief in the inevitable convergence of individual efforts to control and shape the future was articulated by two Frenchmen whose writings had a great influence in the England of the fifties and sixties: the Jesuit Teilhard de Chardin, and the political theorist Bertrand de Jouvenal.

For the interesting fact is that the British intelligentsia —teachers, civil servants, dons and journalists—all stressed that it was 'inevitable' for Britain both to plan and to join E.E.C. Anti-nationalist, anti-imperialist, anti-Little England, indeed, anti-Beaverbrook, these elements might be (*Encounter*, December 1961 and January 1962), but they propelled public opinion irresistably forward. The respected 'father' of post war British planning. Lord Plowden, and Sir Geoffrey Crowther, the chairman of the National Advisory Council for Education in a joint letter to *The Times* on 18 July 1961 said:

> ... with access to the E.E.C. we have the possibility of solving our problems, and maintaining the high standard of living in this island. Without it the prospect before Britain is of being pushed increasingly into a backwater. We shall, no doubt, from our backwater, continue to claim the respect that is due to the leader of the Commonwealth. But if we cannot earn and keep it, it will be an empty title. What good did it do the Sultan of Turkey, in the end, to be the Caliph of Islam.

Having already agreed in 1959 to exchange information with the European Atomic Energy Community, EURATOM (set up at the same time as the Common Market to finance and develop nuclear power for industry in Europe), Britain realised the advantages of promoting research and training of atomic scientists and technologists. This encouraged others to go further. And so a ginger group for bringing Britain in, the Common Market Campaign Committee, was founded by the former British Ambassador to Paris, Sir Gladwyn Jebb (now Lord Gladwyn).

Mr. Macmillan's announcement on 31 July 1961 that Britain was going to open negotiations to join the Common Market was no surprise. But between then and 14 January 1963, when General de Gaulle declared that Britain was not ready for Common Market membership, two events—symptoms both of the position of Britain in the world—took place. One was the Labour Party's condemnation of the move; the other was the Prime Minister's solicitation of the American missile Polaris at Nassau, with the concomitant agreements about America's European umbrella: The North Atlantic Treaty Organisation. France did not want the umbrella to be held by American hands, and Britain still had reservations about the submergence of her identity.

The great irony of all was that the final blow was dealt by the French Foreign Minister, M. Couve de Murville, in making the 'indefinite adjournment' of the negotiations at Brussels on 29 January 1963.

He was a Huguenot.

Massé and English planning

French practice was impinging internally on England too. An American observer describes them as 'suddenly awakened' in 1961 'to an interest in French planning, hoping to find in the techniques a secret of growth that could be applied to the sluggish British economy'. But he added: 'The hope is, unfortunately, doomed to frustration. French planning is in some important respects the opposite of planning.' He compared it to 'a revivalist prayer-meeting', spreading the gospel of expansion, hortatory rather than regulatory (Kindleberger, 1963, 155).

By 1961 France was entering on the fourth of its four post-war plans, drafted by its *Commissariat général du Plan*. So the *Commissaire général*, M. Massé, formerly the Deputy General Manager of *Électricité de France* was invited over in that year to speak at a symposium organised by the National Institute of Economic and Social Research in London. After hearing him J. Christopher Dow, commenting on the fact that the French rate of economic growth was double that of the United Kingdom gave it as his impression that 'many of those who attended the conference came to the conclusion that the French joint planning procedure must have contributed something to France's rapid economic development' (*Planning*, 1961, 208).

Planning in England had long been advocated by Political and Economic Planning (P.E.P.), a pre-war organisation whose initial programme so frightened Aldous Huxley that he left it and wrote *Brave New World* (1931). Thirty years later it carried a special issue on 'Economic Planning in France' (*Planning*, 14 August 1961), reporting M. Massé's address at the National Institute of Economic and Social Research. As Massé outlined it, the administrative structure of the plan had its permanent staff of sixty synthesising the recommendations of twenty-five modernisation committees, each representing a particular industry or activity.

Membership of these committees, consisting of from thirty to fifty persons, was open to business leaders, trade unionists, civil servants or citizens.

In the following year the British Government set up a National Economic Development Council composed of twenty-five members. It was, as a Frenchman says, 'mindful of the French Experiment' (Bauchet, 1964, 19). Sir Robert Hall, himself a negotiator for Britain in Europe, described N.E.D.C. as 'really a decision to adopt the French line' (Bauchet, 1964, 14).

That French 'line' was rapid technological growth based on the exploitation of hydro-electric energy in the

Rhône, the Alps and the Pyrenees (French railways have been electrified), oil in Algiers and natural gas at Lacq. Indeed the latter also yields sulphur as well. Nor is that the only by-product. New ideas in automobile manufacture have enabled Renault to create a new machine tool industry, just as Bull has become an internationally known computer manufacturer.

French aircraft design—evidenced by the Caravelles and the Mystère have led to the formation of an Anglo-French organisation to produce the Concorde.

N.E.D.C. and English adaptations of French technical Training

This expansionist evangel has extended to education. The state schools traditionally based on mathematics and cultivating the national scientific approach, responded. The cul-de-sac of the old primary schools, originally broken open by *classes post-scolaires* for the fifteen and sixteen year olds, have been provided with further exits by the *cours complémentaires*, a three year course that might offer rural or technical courses or even studies analogous to those given in the select *lycées*. Enrolment to these courses has increased by 240 per cent during the period 1945–6 to 1960–1, from 162,000 to 551,522. (The enrolment to primary schools increasing from 3,869,000 to 6,096,867 in the same period) (Wylie, 1963, 178). The *cours complémentaire* is becoming indeed a *collège d'enseignement général.*

Since 1959 the distinction between primary and secondary education has been abolished. All children follow the same course till they are thirteen and, in the last two years, are assessed as to their suitability for one of four further types of course: general education (short or long) and technical training (short or long). Not even these are walled up lanes, as provision is made for crossing over where necessary or desirable.

But it is the *centres d'apprentissage*, now the *collèges*

d'enseignement technique, which have evoked most favourable comment in England. To Lady Williams they are 'France's most significant contribution to training for skill' (Williams, 1963, 85). Three years of practical and theoretical training plus physical education and general studies culminate in an examination for the *Certificat d'Aptitude professionel* (C.A.P.). This can also be obtained from a works school (as run, for instance, by Renault), or by an industrial apprentices' school. Indeed the *collèges* account for up to a third of those preparing to enter skilled trades.

Similarly, artisan training comes under the *Chambres des Métiers*, who administer and examine apprentices in the handicrafts for the *Examen du Fin de l'Apprentissage Artisana* (E.F.A.), after which they can work for *le patronat*.

The late age of beginning apprenticeship (16) and the length (5 years) made Britain unique in Europe, and evoked from Lady Williams the recommendation that the 'quite irrational and almost mystic significance associated with the age of 21' as the age when apprenticeship could be completed, should be abolished (Williams, 1963, 200–4). For, as she pointed out, 'the French F.P.A. system has proved conclusively that, provided selection is carefully made, a man can be trained for skilled work in nine months' (Williams, 1963, 201).

The F.P.A. system to which she referred takes its name from the *Formation Professionelle des Adultes* which is far more comprehensive than the retraining systems offered to adults by other countries. Though it began during the depression in 1936, it was vastly developed after the war to cope with the enormous shortage of skilled manpower. Under *l'Institut National de Formation des Cadres Professionels* (I.N.F.C.P.) over 100 such centres were set up over France, and have so developed that they now offer courses for prospective technicians, *second degré* as well. Administered by employers, workers and the Ministry of Labour, through *l'Association Nationale*

Interprofessionelle pour la Formation Rationale de la Main-d'Oeuvre (A.N.I.F.R.M.D.), it takes over from the age of 17 to 46 anyone who can pass a psychological test and a medical examination. Full family allowances are paid and after nine months the candidate, if successful, obtains a professional certificate, which becomes permanent after they have worked at their trade for another six months.

From the French, the British adopted for their Industrial training Act of 1963 the *taxe d'apprentissage*—a special tax imposed on all industry to provide funds for vocational education—and the industrial training boards, analogous to the *Commissions Nationales Professionelles Consultatives*.

The very passage of the Industrial Training Act was accelerated by the realisation that the Treaty of Rome envisaged all member states of the Common Market establishing a mutually recognised system of industrial training which would enable workers to move freely across national barriers.

The European Technological Community

By 1967 'Americanisation' had overtones more resonantly economic than educational, since, as the French journalist M. Jean-Jacques Servan-Schreiber pointed out, the leading power in Europe by 1982 would be, after America and Russia, America-in-Europe. This thesis, outlined in his *Le Defi Americain* (1967) certainly impressed English supporters of the Common Market, and was used by *The Times* in a leading article on 15 November 1967 to support its argument that "the choice for France and her partners is not just to accept or reject British technological cooperation in a vacuum. It is to accept a genuine widening of the Common Market or leave the European field open to the further encroachment of American industry and influence."

10

Multiformity in uniformity

The minister's watch

That the French minister of public instruction can boast
'that a million boys are saying the same lesson during
the same half-hour in every village and town of France',
has long seemed a joke to English observers of French
education. John Stuart Mill used it in criticising Comte's
proposal that the whole speculative intellect of the human
race should be simultaneously concentrated on one question at a time (Mill, 1865, 181–2). The minister's remark
(credited to Hippolyte Fortoul) has been repeated with
variations till our own time.

But, as Matthew Arnold observed, it was not so much
that all French boys should be saying the same lesson
at the same time, as the relevance of *what* they were
saying. Multiformity might be a greater evil than uniformity (Arnold, 1904, 174–5). Clive Bell also used the
French system to illuminate the 'smug and hypocritical'
and 'grossly and at bottom so brutal' nature of English
civilisation which ensured 'that even a first-rate Englishman necessarily becomes an outlaw' (Bell, 1928, 80-2).
He saw the 'well-oiled whetstone' of French education
'gently obliterating the rough corners of the French boy',
who becomes, 'daily more conscious of his solidarity with
his accomplices in a peculiar and gracious secret',
whereas his English counterpart, especially if possessed

of a fine sensibility, finds himself 'from the outset at loggerheads with the world in which he is to live'.

This centralisation has made it easier for the French to devise a coherent system of anticipating the educational consequences of planned economic growth, a problem now facing Britain. Thus M. Fourastié anticipates 'une scolarisation de 85 per cent des jeunes de dix-sept et dix-huit ans' by 1985. He epitomises the combination of technical competence, persuasion and pressure that characterises the commissariat du plan.

Just as France set the pace in the development of the kilowatt-hour by installing the first electric lights in London, so now she is setting the pace in the prevision of its social consequences. Educationally they involve what Louis Cros has called *L'explosion scolaire*. This 'explosion' can be seen in the Fifth French Plan. The percentage of the age group acquiring the *baccalauréat* will be raised to 30 per cent in 1972 and to 40–45 per cent in 1985. (This should be compared to the 15 per cent in 1965, 1 per cent in 1915 and ·05 per cent in 1850).

Such 'indicative' planning greatly impressed the Robbins Committee, appointed by the Prime Minister to consider the future of higher education in Britain. After visiting France in February 1962, it reported:

It is not so much the present state of educational affairs in France that has significance in Great Britain (although there are features of it to be envied) as the imaginative plans adopted for the future. To say that there is a possibility that the situation in 1970 will in certain respects fall short of the French government's current plans is not to detract from the importance of the fact that these plans now exist, and that steps are being taken to put them into effect (Cmnd. 2154—v, 1964, 57).

Noting that the rate of university expansion in France since the war had been twice that of Britain (attributable to a sharper rise in the birth rate) and that the numbers taking the *baccalauréat* would treble between 1958/9 and

1968/9, the Robbins Committee also indicated that in secondary education the French paid more deference to parental wishes in the selection for secondary education at thirteen than the British did at eleven. It also noted the school leaving age would be raised to sixteen before it was raised in Britain. Even though the greater wastage rate of students in French higher education might offset all these advantages, yet the committee admitted 'the position might be reversed' by 1970 if the French plans were realised.

The baccalauréat and G.C.E.

In the field of university entrance in Britain recent discussions seem to be leaning to, if not learning from, recent changes in the French *baccalauréat*. The *baccalauréat* (itself possible only under a centralised system), is, compared to its English counterpart, the 'A' levels of the G.C.E., encyclopaedist-generalist, since it obliges students to study in several fields. This will continue after 1967 when five types of *baccalauréat*, known as A, B, C, D, and T, will be established. All of them will have common elements like philosophy, French, History (except T), a foreign language and physical education, in addition to their particular specialisms.

The *baccalauréat* also reflects the unification of science, personified in the Institut. Though after 1967 Arts students will be able to dispense with Science, they will still have to sit for six subjects, whilst science students will have to study Philosophy, French, History, Geography and Modern Languages. All subjects are examined both orally and in writing.

Organised by the Ministry which defines the syllabus with the aid of specialist committees and publishes it in the *Journal Officielle*, the *baccalauréat* caters for the particular needs of the north and the south. Compared to the eight British examining boards, it has a uniformity which is quite admirable since the time at which it is taken, its validity and its uniform marking has, and will be, governed from the centre. Indeed, this central control will, if anything, be firmer after 1967, since only those who score marks of over 50 per cent will be allowed to go forward to universities. Those below this level but who score above 40 per cent in the examination will be awarded the *certificat de fin d'études secondaires.*

Concomitantly, from 1966 onwards, all children from 11 to 16 will go to comprehensive schools where selection and guidance will take place at the upper end. As a result of this the *lycée*, hitherto the counterpart of the grammar school, will become a sixth form college. An alternative institution for those not so destined will be the *college d'enseignement général.*

Lastly the number of educational districts or academies (and therefore of state universities) has increased to 23. After 1968 only the students who possess the C, D, or T *baccalauréat* will qualify for entrance to the science faculties; holders of the other types of *baccalauréat* who wish to enter these faculties may only do so after special permission or after passing a special examination.

The raising of standards in the *baccalauréat* may diminish the number—some thousand odd—of assistants at present teaching in English schools since they may have to stay at home to sit their *baccalauréat.* At the same time to secure greater uniformity in entrance requirements for British universities, the Schools Council and the Standing Conference on University Entrance have produced sets of proposals which both involve planning, in French fashion, the school curriculum on a modular basis.

Anglo-French groups

As the most popular foreign language in English schools, offered by some 86,888 pupils at ordinary level in 1962, and 12,454 at advanced level, French has no rivals. The corresponding figures for German are 14,324, at 'O' level and 3,725 at 'A'.

Reasons for this can be found in the foregoing pages, but two further ones can be found in the structure of language teaching in England. For teachers of French have a tradition of co-operation that goes back over a century when an association of French teachers in England was organised by M. Boulland under the auspices of the College of Preceptors (Schaible, 1863, 4). There were then about 500 potential members in the country. Thirty years later in 1891, a Franco-English guild was founded by Miss Williams, a graduate of the University of Paris, a lecturer at the training college of Sèvres and Fontenay. Originally for young women who wish to extend their knowledge of English it soon embraced students of other nationalities, and attracted the official support of Ferdinand Buisson, Director of Primary Education, and after 1897, of the Sorbonne. The English Board of Education began to send intending teachers of French and so did certain American universities. It then changed its name to the International Guild.

The second reason lies in the 'civic' and 'new' universities. The first endowment for a civic institution of higher education—that made by H. R. Hartley for Southampton in 1843—came from a former wine-merchant who spent most of his time in France, and the first classes held in it were in French—in 1863. In subsequent 'civic' foundations French was also a strong subject from the beginning. After 'day training colleges' were opened in them after 1890, French rapidly became one of the monoliths of their Faculties of Arts, fostered by groups like the Entente Cordiale Society formed in 1896, the Association of Great Britain and France (founded by the Federation of British Industries in 1917) and the Anglo-French Society (formed in 1919 by M. Henri Davray). They joined together after the first world war, and during the second—in 1944—were collectively rechristened the Franco-British Society. This provides, through its journal *Britain-France* (after 1965 the *Journal of the Franco-British Society*), a forum for local groups and information about French books, especially the *Livres de Poche* which, said one of its reviewers have exerted an 'incalculable and exciting influence. For never before have French books at a modest price been so widely accessible, or one might add, so freshly guillotined. With its French counterpart, The association *France-Grande Bretagne* (formed in 1901) it promotes joint conferences.

Schemes for teaching assistants to exchange between the two countries, have been supplemented by the provision of English *moniteurs* for the *colonies de vacances*, a scheme itself adopted in England. The diploma they take is the result of co-operation between universities of Lille, London and Edinburgh.

The 'new' universities of Britain with their accent on schools of study, rather than departments, have reflected the trend, visible elsewhere, for European integration. Indeed, before they were founded, M. Anthonin Besse made a substantial donation to the University of Oxford in 1948 to stimulate an interest in the study of the continent and to provide easier access for Frenchmen at Oxford. This resulted in the foundation of St. Anthony's College.

Since 1963 a 'Britain in Europe' movement has been launched under the Presidency of Lord Gladwyn, who obligingly provided its credo, *The European Idea* (1966). A Wider Europe Committee was also formed in June 1965 by some Labour backbenchers. 'Wider' in its case meant 'from the Atlantic to the Urals' (*The Guardian*, 3 June 1965).

L'Europe fraternelle

For 'Europe from the Atlantic to the Urals' is a logical extension of *l'Europe européene;* it is indeed *l'Europe fraternelle*. This *l'Europe fraternelle* is however a kind of Eurotechnocracy, and many suspect that in joining it 'we might be opening the door wide in Europe to blindly competitive technology and supernatural bureaucracies remote from democratic control'. So they argue 'if the primary aim is really to place Britain in a larger community in recognition of the dominant place of science and technology in the shaping of nations; the more obvious union to seek would be with the U.S.' (Calder, 1967).

To others the very antiquity of French suggestions for a United States of Europe evokes suspicion. From the time of Sully (1603), Emeric Crucé (1623), the Abbé de St. Pierre (1713), Rousseau (1761), St. Simon (1802) to Monnet (1946) such schemes have led the English to abreact into nationalism. Such abreaction depressed Matthew Arnold who lamented England's failure to perceive how 'the world is going, and must go, and preparing herself accordingly'.

Subsequent English intellectuals have echoed his views. Seventy-seven of them, polled by *Encounter* in 1963, declared for entry into the Common Market. Only 17 were against, and 16 indifferent. A more broadly-based sample of the public, according to *New Society* in June 1966, yielded the information that though 60 per cent of the adult population would like to join the E.E.C. for economic reasons, France and Germany and Italy ranked very low as 'trustable' countries, obtaining only 35, 38 and 39 per cent of the sample votes, as compared with the 87, 73 and 71 per cent for Australia, Sweden and the U.S.A.

Suspicion survives of French 'rayonnement' (dispersal of French culture and technology) over an area extending beyond the traditional frontiers of Europe to Africa and the Middle East as envisaged by De Gaulle. By 1966, when the Soviet Union adopted the French system of colour television in place of the American, it looked a realistic dream.

France's traditional 'mission' involves considering Europe as a third 'arena' in which neither America nor the East would have a controlling interest (Pickles, 1966, 126). It also involves resistance to being 'colonised' by

American investment. So France provides government aid to increase industrial efficiency, buys gold, opts out of the North Atlantic Treaty Organisation, and refuses to endorse American actions in foreign fields.

This, as much as anything, has posed two major surrenders for Britain. The first is the surrender of the American nuclear umbrella and of the 'special relationship' with America. Often spelt out, most recently by a collective letter from American university Chancellors and Presidents in *The Times* of 21 February 1967, this 'special relationship' is most offensive since it is a reminder to De Gaulle of his earlier exclusion from Yalta and Potsdam, and his 'invitation' to San Francisco. These wounds, as Mrs. Pickles said 'can be felt afresh with any change in Franco-British weather' (1966, 4). It has led France to make progressive overtures to Eastern Europe to enlarge the boundaries of the 'Little Europe' of the six E.E.C. countries to ensure that it is the equal of the U.S.A. The second British surrender is of the key of the commonwealth pantry, a surrender which would increase her balance of payments deficit by £100m. a year (Hansard, 2 June 1965).

But the American umbrella and the Commonwealth pantry may not be quite as exclusively determinist as the cynics might suppose. The Anglo-French agreement in November 1962 to set up joint management and planning procedures to build the Concorde aircraft; the resuscitation in 1957 of the scheme first proposed in 1802 and begun in 1872 to construct a channel tunnel; the purchase of French gas from North Africa for the English grid; the popularity of real and fictional French figures (Brigitte Bardot and Maigret) on film and television screens indicate a continuous economic and cultural pull.

'Où allons-nous?' asked the French economist Victor Cambon in a book of that name in 1919. A year later he gave the answer in *L'Industrie organisée, d'après les méthodes américaines* (1920). For France has become a technocracy in a wider sense even than the Americans, who invented that word in 1919, imagined. Gold may not have been abandoned in favour of a currency based on energy certificates, but her polytechnicians and *normaliens* are a real functional élite, who play 'a much greater part in the policy making process and in day-to-day administration than they do in Britain' (Ridley-Blondel, 1964, 56–7).

Here, it seems, the lesson has been learned. An ever increasing number of Englishmen are braving the three foreign language requirement for entry to the *Institut Européen d'Administration des Affaires*, France's prestigious nine year old business school housed in the palace of Fontainebleau, recently described as 'fast challenging Harvard's position as the top training ground of Europe's top management' (*Sunday Times*, 18 June 1967, 16).

Speaking at Scarborough in 1963 in the famous 'science debate' at the Labour Party Conference of that year, Mr. Harold Wilson said farewell to 'the days of the old-boy network approach to life' with its belief that 'a special relationship with someone or other' would 'bail us out'. Instead he hailed the new socialism by announcing that 'in the Cabinet room and the board room alike those charged with the control of our affairs must be ready to think and speak in the language of our scientific age' (Wilson, 1964, 28).

In this scientific age France is still setting precedents. The Schools Council, in some of its symposia on the aims of education indicates this. Others are continuing the work of Matthew Arnold, George Saintsbury and Lytton Strachey. English social work has learned from the Abbé Godin and his 'worker priests', English life from the existential insights of Sartre. English pageantry has been revived by the *Son et Lumière*. For France is the true home of humanism. 'I conceive myself,' wrote Sartre, 'both as totally free and as unable to prevent the fact that the meaning of the world comes to it from myself' (Bree and Guiton, 1957, 5).

To be able to say that in so centralised a country is wholly French.

Guide to further reading

ADAMSON, J. W., *English Education 1789–1902*. Cambridge University Press, 1930.

AGNEW, D. C., *Protestant Exiles from France in the Reign of Louis XIV*, 3rd Edition, Edinburgh, 1886.

ALBERT-SOREL, J., *Histoire de France et d'Angleterre, La Rivalité de l'Entente*, Holland: Les Editions Française d'Amsterdam. n.d.

ALEXANDER E., *Matthew Arnold and John Stuart Mill*, London: Routledge & Kegan Paul, 1965.

ALGER, J. G., *English Caricature & Satire on Napoleon*, London, 1884.

ALGER, J. G., *Englishmen in the French Revolution*, London, 1889.

ALGER, J. G., *Napoleon's British Visitors and Captives 1801–1815*, London, 1904.

ALLBUT, SIR T. CLIFFORD, 'Palissy, Bacon and the revival of Natural Science', *Proceedings of the British Academy*, vi, 1914.

Annales de la Société Jean Jacques Rousseau, Geneva, 1905.

ARNOLD, M., *Mixed Essays*, London: Smith & Evans, 1904.

ARON, RAYMOND, *France: Steadfast and Changing*. Cambridge, Mass.: Harvard University Press, 1960.

ARTZ, F. B., *The Development of French Technical Education 1500–1850*, Boston: M.I.T. Press, 1966.

ASHTON, J., *English Caricature and Satire on Napoleon I*, London, 1884.

AUDIGANE, A., 'Du mouvement intellectuel parmi les populations ouvrières'. *Revue des Deux Mondes*, x, 1851, 860–93.

AUSTEN-LEIGH, R. A., 'Montpellier and its Associations', *Proceedings of the Huguenot Society*, xvii, No. 2, 1943, 122–144.

AUSTEN-LEIGH, R. A., 'The Family of Chenevix', *P.H.J.*, xvii, 1945, 311–329.

BAILEY, R., '45 Million Frenchmen', *Spectator*, 1960.

BALDENSPERGER, F., *Le mouvement des idées dans l'émigration française 1789-1815*, Paris, 1925.

BALL, W. W. R., *History of the study of Mathematics at Cambridge*, Cambridge University Press, 1889.

BALLANTYNE, A., *Voltaire's Visit to England 1726–1729*, London: John Murray, 1919.

BAR, P., *P. Budin*, Paris, 1907.

BARET, R., 'Bibliographie critique sur les relations du gouverne-
ment brittanique avec les émigrés et les royalistes de l'Ouest',
La Province du Maine, xv, 177–186, 1934.

BARNARD, H. C., *The French Tradition in Education*, Cambridge
University Press, 1929.

BARRY, F. V. (ed.), *Maria Edgeworth. Chosen Letters*, London:
Jonathan Cape, 1931, 181.

BASTIDE, CHARLES, *The Anglo-French Entente in the Seventeenth
Century*, London: John Lane, 1914.

BAUCHET, P., *Economic Planning. The French Experience*, translated by Daphne Woodward, London: Heinemann, 1964.

BEER, E. S. DE,, 'The Revocation of the Edict of Nantes and
English Public Opinion', *P.H.S.*, xviii, 1950, 292–310.

BELOFF, N., *The General Says No*, Harmondsworth, Middlesex:
Penguin Books, 1963.

BELL, C., *Civilisation*, London: Chatto & Windus, 1928.

BLISS, A. J., *A Dictionary of Foreign Words and Phrases in
Current English*, London: Routledge & Kegan Paul, 1966.

BIGBY, D. A., *Anglo-French Relations 1641–1649*, London:
University of London Press, 1933.

BOESIGER and GIRSBERGER, (ed.), *Le Corbusier 1910–1960*, Zurich
and Stuttgart, 1960.

BOLGAR, R. R., 'Victor Cousin and Nineteenth Century Education', *Cambridge Journal*, ii, 1948–9, 357 & 8.

BONNO, G., 'La Culture et la civilisation britanniques devant
l'opinion française de la paix d'Utrecht aux Lettres philosophiques', *Transactions of the American Philosophical
Society*, xxxviii, 1948, 14–15.

BOURCHENIN, P. D., *Études sur les Académies Protestantes en
France aux XVIe et XVIIe Siècles*, Paris: Grassart, 1894.

BOYCE, G. C., *The English-German Nation in the University of
Paris during the Middle Ages*, Bruges, 1927.

BOYD, W., *The 'Émile' of Jean-Jacques Rousseau*, New York:
Teachers College, 1962.

BOYD, W., *The Minor Writings of Jean-Jacques Rousseau*, New
York: Teachers College, 1962.

BRACQ, J. C., *France under the Republic*, New York: C. Scribner's
Sons, 1910.

BRADLEY, H., *The Making of English*, London: Macmillan, 1904.

BRAMSTED, E., 'The Six: Attitudes and Institutions, 1946–63', in

Bell, C. (ed.), *Europe without Britain. Six Studies of Britain's Application to join the Common Market and its Breakdown*, Melbourne: F. W. Cheshire for the A.I.I.A., 1963.

BRAUER, G. C., *The Education of a Gentleman*, New York: Bookman Associates, 1959.

BREE, G., and GUITON, M., *An Age of Fiction*, New Brunswick: Rutgers University Press, 1959.

BROWN, P. A., *The French Revolution in English History*, London: Crosby Lockwood & Son, 1918.

BUCHANAN, J. Y., 'The Royal Society', *Nature*, Vol. 69, 1904, 293.

BULWER, SIR E. L., *Works*, London, 1840.

BURNS, J. S., *The History of the French, Walloon Dutch and other Foreign Protestant Refugees settled in England*, London, 1846.

BURNS, J. H., 'Bentham and the French Revolution', *Transaction of the Royal Historical Society*, 5th Series, xvi, 1966, 95–114.

BURY, J. P. T. and BARRY, J. C., *An Englishman in Paris 1803*, The Journal of Bertie Greatheed London: Geoffrey Bles, 1953.

BUSCOT, CANON, W., *History of Cotton College, 1763–1873*, London: Burns, Oates & Washbourne, 1940.

BUSSEY, G. C., *Man a machine—La Mettrie*, Chicago, 1927.

CALDER, N., 'Is Eurotech the Answer?', *New Statesman and Nation*, 3 February, 1967, 140.

CAMERON, R. E., *France and the Economic Development of Europe*, Princeton University Press, 1961.

CAMPOS, C., *The View of France from Arnold to Bloomsbury*, London: Oxford University Press, 1965.

CAPLAT, G., L'Administration de l'éducation nationale et la réforme administrative, Paris: Berger-Levrault, 1960.

CARDON, G., *La Fondation de l'Université de Douai*, Paris, 1892.

CARDWELL, D. F. L., *The Organisation of Science in England*, London: Heinemann, 1951.

CAUTE, DAVID, *Communism and the French Intellectuals 1914–1960*, London: Andre Deutsch, 1964.

CHADWICK, N. H., 'Intellectual Contacts between Britain and Gaul in the Fifth Century', *Studies in Early British History*, Cambridge University Press, 1954, 189–263.

CHALONER, W. H., 'Dr Joseph Priestley, John Wilkinson and the French Revolution 1789–1802', *Transactions of the Royal Historical Society*, 5th Series, vii, 1958, 21–40.

CHAMBERLAIN, NEIL W., *Private and Public Planning*, London: McGraw-Hill Book Company, 1965.

CHARLANNE, *L'influence française en Angleterre au XVIIe Siècle*, Paris, 1906.

CLOVER, B., *The Mastery of the French Language in England*, New York, 1888.

COBBAN, A., (ed.), *The Debate on the French Revolution 1789–1800*, London: Nicholas Kaye, 1950.

COCHIN, A., *La révolution et la libre pensée*, Paris, 1924.

COLEBY, L. J., *The Chemical Studies of P. J. Macquer*, London: George Allen & Unwin, 1930.

COLLINS, R. W., *Catholicism and the Second French Republic 1848–1852*, New York: Columbia University Press, 1923.

COLVILLE, ALFRED, and TEMPERLEY, HAROLD, *Studies in Anglo-French History during the Eighteenth, Nineteenth and Twentieth Centuries*, Cambridge University Press, 1935.

COUILLING, S. M. B., 'Renan's influence on Matthew Arnold's Political and Social Criticism', *Florida State University Studies*, 5, 1952.

COURTAULD, S. A., 'East Anglia and the Huguenot Textile Industry', *P.H.S.*, xiii, No. 2, 1924, 125–153.

CROS, L., *L'Explosion Scolaire*, Paris: S.E.V.P.E.N., 1961.

CRU, R. L., *Diderot as a Disciple of English Thought*, New York, 1913.

CULLER, D. D., *The Imperial Intellect. A Study of Newman's Ideal*, Yale University Press, 1955.

CUMMING, IAN, *Helvetius: His Life and Place in the History of Educational Thought*, London: Routledge & Kegan Paul, 1955.

CUNNINGHAM, W., *Alien Immigrants to England*, London, 1897.

DARWIN, E., *A Plan for the Conduct of Female Education in Boarding Schools*, 1797, 115–117.

DAVIES, S. J., *The Education of Engineers in some European Countries*, A.T.I. Paper, February, 1953.

DAVY, M. J. B., *Interpretive History of Flight*, London: H.M.S.O., 1948.

DÉSMOLINS, E., *Anglo-Saxon Superiority: To What is it due?* London, 1899.

DEVONSHIRE, M. G., *The English Novel in France*, London: University of London Press, 1929.

Dictionary of National Biography 1931–1940, Oxford: Clarendon Press, 1949.

DOBINSON, C. H., *Technical Education for Adolescents*, London: Harrap, 1951.

DORMOY, M., *L'Architecture Française*, Paris, 1938.

DURKHEIM, E., *L'Évolution Pedagogique en France*, Paris, 1938.

DUFLOU, G., *L'Université d'Oxford et son Enseignement des Langues modernes*, Ghent, 1894.

DUVEAU, G., *Les Instituteurs*, Paris: Éditions du Seuil, 1957.

Economist, The, 'Planning like the French', 28 October, 1961.

EDGEWORTH, R. L., *Memoirs*, 1821, i, 221.

Encounter, A Symposium 'Going into Europe', December 1962 and January 1963.

ESDAILE, K. A., 'The Part Played by Refugee Sculptors 1600–1750', *P.H.S.*, xviii, No. 3, 1949, 254–262.

ESPINASSE, F., *Literary Recollections and Sketches*, London, 1893.

ETIEMBLE, R., *Parlez-vous frangáis?*, Paris: Gallimard, 1964.

EVANS, J., 'Huguenot Goldsmiths in England and Ireland', *P.H.S.*, xiv, 4, 1933, 496–554.

FAIRCLOUGH, G. T., 'A Fugitive and Gracious Light. The Relation of Joseph Joubert to Matthew Arnold's Thought', *University of Nebraska Studies, New Series*, No. 23, Lincoln, Nebraska, 1961.

FALCUCCI, C., *L'Humanisme dans l'enseignement secondaire en France au dix-neuvième Siècle*, Paris, 1939.

FARMER, P., *France Reviews its Revolutionary Origins*, New York: Octagon Books, 1963.

FARRER, L. E., *La Vie et les Oeuvres de Claude Sainliens*, Paris: Honoré Champion, 1908.

FARRINGTON, F. E., *The Public Primary School System of France*, London: Longmans, Green, 1906.

FIRTH, SIR C., *Modern Languages at Oxford 1724–1929*, London: Oxford University Press, 1929.

FLEMING, J. A., *Flemish Influence in Britain*, Glasgow: Jackson, Wylie & Co., 1930, 2 vols.

FONTENELLE, B. LE B., *Histoire du renouvellement de l'Académie Royale des Sciences en Oeuvres*, vol. viii, Paris, 1715.

FOSTER, SIR M., 'Address', *Report of the British Association for the Advancement of Science 1899*, London, 1900.

FOWLER, H. W., *A Dictionary of Modern English Usage*, Oxford: Clarendon Press, 1937.

FRANKEL, C., *The Faith of reason: the idea of Progress in the French enlightenment*, New York, 1948.

GALTON, F., *English Men of Science*, London, 1874, 253, quoted Pearson, *op. cit.*, ii, 155.

GARDINER, D., *English Girlhood at School*, London: Oxford University Press, 1929, 354–5.

GLATIGNY, M., *Histoire de l'Enseignement en France*, Paris, 1949.

GREEN, F. C., *A Comparative View of French and British Civilisation, 1850–1870*, London: J. M. Dent and Sons, 1965.

GREENWOOD, MAJOR, *Some Pioneers of Social Medicine*, Heath Clark Lectures 1946, London: Oxford University Press, 1948, 106.

GREER, D., *The Incidence of the Emigration during the French Revolution*, Cambridge: Harvard University Press, 1951.

GUÉHENNO, *Jean-Jacques Rousseau*, translated by Doreen and John Weightman, London: Routledge & Kegan Paul, 1966.

GUYAU, M. J., *La genèse de l'idée de temps*, Paris, 1902.

GUYOT, R., *La Première Entente Cordiale*, Paris: F. Rieder et Cie, 1926.

GWYNN, R., *Lord Shrewsbury, Pugin and the Catholic Revival*, London: Hollis and Carter, 1946.

HAAS, E. B., 'Technocracy, Pluralism and the New Europe' in Stephen R. Graubard (ed.), *A New Europe?*, Boston: 1964, 62–89.

HAAS, E. B., *Beyond the Nation-State*, Stanford University Press, 1964.

HACKETT, J., and A. M., *Economic Planning in France*, London: George Allen and Unwin, 1963.

HALL, SIR R., *Rede Lecture on Planning*, Cambridge University Press, 1962.

HARDING, F. J. W., *Matthew Arnold the Critic and France*, Geneva: Libraire Droz, 1964.

HARRISON, FREDERIC, *Autobiographic Memoirs*, vol. ii, London: Macmillan, 1911.

HARRISON CHURCH, R. J., 'The French School of Geography' in Griffith Taylor (ed.) *Geography in the Twentieth Century*, London: Methuen, 1962.

HATJE, G. (ed.), *Encyclopaedia of Modern Architecture*, London: Thames and Hudson, 1963 .

HAUSERMANN, H. W., *The Genevese Background*, London: George Allen and Unwin, 1952.

HAYES, R., *Ireland and Irishmen in the French Revolution*, London: Ernest Benn, 1922.

HAZEN, C. D., *Contemporary American Opinion on the French Revolution*, Baltimore: Johns Hopkins University Studies in Historical and Political Science Extra, vol. xvii, 1897.

HEAD, SIR F., *A Faggot of French Sticks*, London, 1852.

HEAVISIDE, O., 'The French Academy', *Nature*, vol. 69, 1904, 317.

HEDGCOCK, D., *Garrick et ses amis françaises*, Paris, 1911.

H.M.S.O., *Higher Education. Appendix Five to the Report of the Committee appointed by the Prime Minister under the Chairmanship of Lord Robbins, 1961–63. Higher Education in Other Countries*. Cmnd. 2154, V, 1964.

HIPPEAU, C., *L'instruction publique en France pendant la Révolution: Discours et Rapports*, Paris, 1881.

HITCHCOCK, H. R., *The Crystal Palace*, Northampton, Mass., 1952; *Early Victorian Architecture in Britain. The Early Phase 1835–1855*, London: Architectural Press, 1955.

HOFFMAN, S., KINDLEBERGER, C. P., WYLIE, L., PITTS, J. R., DUROSELLE, J. B., and GOGUEL, F., *France: Change and Tradition*, London: Victor Gollancz, 1963.

HOLMES, U. T., JR., 'Transactions in European Education' in Reynolds, Robert; Clagett, Marshall; Post, Gaines; *Twelfth Century Europe and the Foundations of Modern Society*, University of Wisconsin Press, 1961.

HOWARTH, O. J. R., *The British Association:* a retrospect, London: British Association, 1931.

HUNKIN, P., *Enseignement et politique en France et en Angleterre*, Paris: Institut Pedagogique National, 1962.

HURLBUT, W. H. *France and the Republic: a Record of things seen and learned in the French Provinces during the Centennial year 1889*, London: Longmans Green & Co., 1890.

HUSZAR, GEORGE B. DE (ed.), *The Intellectuals: A Controversial Portrait*, Glencoe: Free Press, 1960.

HUVELIN, P., 'Planning in France', *Review of the Federation of British Industries*, April, 1962.

JERROLD, W. B., *On the Boulevards*, London, 1867.

JOHNSON, D., *Guizot. Aspects of French History 1787–1874*, London: Routledge & Kegan Paul, 1963.

KELLY, T., *George Birkbeck*, Liverpool University Press, 1957.

KEYNES, J. M., 'Francis Ysidro Edgeworth', *Economic Journal*, March 1926, 151.

KINDLEBERGER, C. P., *Economic Growth in France and Britain*, Cambridge: Harvard University Press, 1964.

KIRWAN, A. V., 'Modern France: Its Journalism (1863)', *Saturday Review*, xiv, 1869, 535–6.

KLEIMANN, R., *Atlantic Crises. American Diplomacy Confronts a Resurgent Europe*, London: Sidgwick and Jackson, 1965.

KOGAN, H., *The Great E.B.: the Story of the Encyclopaedia Britannica*, Chicago: University Press, 1958.

KRAMER, EDNA E., *The Main Stream of Mathematics*, London: Oxford University Press, 1951.

LAMBERT, R. S., *The Grand Tour*, London: Faber and Faber, 1928.

LAMBLEY, K., *The Teaching and Cultivation of the French Language in England during Tudor and Stuart Times*, Manchester University Press, 1920.

LANDES, D. A., 'French Entrepreneurship and Industrial Growth in the XIXth Century', *Journal of Economic History*, May 1949, 49–61.

LANE POOLE, R., *A History of the Huguenots of the Dispersion*, Oxford, 1880, 73–113.

LAPRADE, W. T., *England and the French Revolution, 1789–1797*, Johns Hopkins University Studies in History and Political Science, xxvii, Baltimore, 1909, 152.

LAYAR, F., 'The Huguenots in North Britain', *P.H.S.*, 111.

LEACH, A. F., *Schools of Medieval England*, London: Methuen, 1915.

LE CORBUSIER, *The Modular: A Harmonious measure to the human scale, universally applicable to architecture and mechanics*, London: Faber, 1954.

LEE, SIR SIDNEY, 'The Beginning of French Translation from the English', *Transactions of the Bibliographical Society*, viii, 1904–6, 85–112.

LEE, SIR SIDNEY, *The French Renaissance in England*, Oxford: Clarendon Press, 1910.

LEGGE, M. D., *Anglo-Norman in the Cloisters*, Edinburgh: Oliver & Boyd, 1950; *Anglo-Norman Literature and its Background*, Edinburgh: Oliver & Boyd, 1962.

LEGOUIS, E., and CAZAMIAN, L., *A History of English Literature*, London: J. M. Dent and Sons, 1928.

LE PATOUREL, J., 'The Treaty of Bretigny 1360', *Transactions of the Royal Historical Society*, 5th Series, x, 1960, 19–40.

LEWIS, M., *Napoleon and His British Captives*, London: George Allen & Unwin, 1967.

LOCKYER, SIR N., 'The Influence of Brain Power on History', *Report of the British Association for the Advancement of Science 1903*, 1904.

LÜTHY, HERBERT, 'The French Intellectuals' in Huszar (q.v.) 444–458.

MACÉ, VICTOR, *La ligue de l'Enseignement*, Paris, 1890.

MCCLELLAND, V. A., *Cardinal Manning. His Public Life and Influence*, Oxford, 1962, 75.

MCCLELLAND, V. A., 'The Kensington Scheme', *The Month*, March 1965, 173–182.

MCCALL, SIR R., 'The Huguenots in Kent', *P.H.S.*, xiii, No. 1, 1924, 18–31.

MCCONNELL, A. J., 'The Dublin Mathematical School in the First Half of the Nineteenth Century', *Proceedings of the Royal Irish Academy*, 50, 1944–5.

MCKAY, D. V., 'Colonialism in the French Geographical Movement 1871–1881', *Geographical Review*, 1943, 24–32.

MACAULAY, J. M., (ed.), *John Anderson, Pioneer of Technical Education and the College he founded by Professor James Muir*, Glasgow : John Smith, 1950.

Macmillan's Magazine, March 1864, 'Concerning the Organisation of Literature', ix, 426–36.

DE LA MAHOTIÈRE, S. R., *The Common Market*, London : Hodder and Stoughton, 1962.

MAIRET, P., *Pioneer of Sociology. The Life and Letters of Patrick Geddes*, London : Lund Humphries, 1957.

MAITLAND, F. W., 'Anglo-French Law Language', *Year Books of Edward II*, 1913.

MANCHÉE, W. H., 'The Fouberts and their Royal Academy', *P.H.S.*, xvi, No. 1, 1938, 77–97.

MANDER, J., *Great Britain or Little England*, London : Secker & Warburg, 1964.

MARCHAND, J., (ed.), *A Frenchman in England: 1784 being the Mélangues sur l'Angleterre' de François de la Rochefoucauld*, translated by S. C. Roberts, Cambridge University Press, 1933.

MARTIN, K., *French Liberal thought in the Eighteenth Century*, London : Ernest Benn, 1929.

MASSON, P. M., *Rousseau et la restauration religieuse*, Paris, 1916.

MAXWELL, C., *The English Traveller in France 1698–1815*, London : Routledge & Kegan Paul, 1932.

MAYER, J., 'Science' in Julian Park (ed.), *The Culture of France in our Time*, Ithaca : Cornell University Press, 1954.

MEAD, W. E., *The Grand Tour in the Eighteenth Century*, Boston, 1914.

MEGRINE, B., *La question scolaire en France*. 'Que sais-je ?', 864, P.U.F., 1946–8.

METRAUX, R., and MEAD, M., *Themes in French Culture*, Stanford University Press, 1954.

MEUNIER, L. A., *La lutte du principe clérical et du principe laïque dans l'enseignement*, Paris, 1861.

MILL, J. S., *Auguste Comte and Positivism 1865*, University of Michigan Press, 1961.

MILL, J. S., *Autobiography*, Oxford : World's Classics, No. 262, 1963.

MILLER, J. B. D., 'Britain without Europe', in Coral Bell, q.v.

MINEKA, F. E., *The Earlier Letters of John Stuart Mill 1812–1848*, London : Routledge & Kegan Paul, 1963.

MINET, W., 'History of the Leicester Fields Church', *P.H.S.*, xiii, 5, 1928, 474–487; 6, 1929, 596–612.

MITCHELL, HARVEY, *The Underground War against Revolutionary France*, Oxford : Clarendon Press, 1965.

MONNET, J., *Les États Unis ont Commencés*, Paris, 1955.

MOODY, T. W., and BECKETT, J. C., *Queen's Belfast 1845–1949*, London : Faber, 1959.

MOORE, DR. JOHN, *View of Society and Manners in France, Switzerland and Germany*, London : 1779, 9th edition London 1800, I, 289.

MOTT, L. A., 'Renan and Matthew Arnold', *Modern Language Notes*, xxxiii, 1918.

MUELLER, I. W., *John Stuart Mill and French Thought*, University of Illinois, 1956.

MUSGRAVE, G., *Ramble through Normandy*, London, 1855.

MUIR, J., John Anderson : *Pioneer of Technical Education*. Ed. by James Macaulay, Glasgow : John Smith & Son, 1950.

MYRDAL, G., *Beyond the Welfare State*, Yale University Press, 1960.

NEF, J. U., *Industry and Government in France and England 1540–1640*, Ithaca, New York : Great Seal Books, 1957. Originally published in the *Memoirs* of the *American Philosophical Society*, xv, 1940.

NEWMAN, J. H., *My Campaign in Ireland*, ed. W. P. Neville, (privately printed Aberdeen 1896).

NICOLSON, H., *The Age of Reason*, London : Constable, 1960.

ORR, J., *English deism: its roots and its fruits*, University of Michigan Press, Michigan, 1934.

ORR, J., *Impact of French upon English*, Oxford University Press, 1948.

OWEN, J. B., *Lectures and Sermons*, London, 1873.

OWEN, L. V. D., *The Connection between England and Burgundy during the first half of the Fifteenth Century*, Oxford: Blackwell, 1909.

PADLEY, R., 'The beginnings of the British Alkali Industry', *University of Birmingham Historical Journal*, iii, 1951, 64–78.

PAGE, W., (ed.), *Letters of Denization and Acts of Naturalisation for Aliens in England*, 1509–1603.

PANKHURST, R. P. K., 'Anna Wheeler: A pioneer Socialist, Feminist and Cooperator', *Political Quarterly*, 1954, xxv, No. 2, 132–143.

PANKHURST, R. P. K., *The Saint Simonians, Mill and Carlyle: A Preface to Modern Thought*, London: Sidgwick and Jackson, 1957.

PARKS, G. B., 'Travel as Education' in *The Seventeenth Century: Studies in the History of English Thought and Literature from Bacon to Pope*, Stanford University Press, 1951.

PARTRIDGE, E., *The French Romantics' Knowledge of English Literature*, Paris: Librairie ancienne Édouard Champion, 1924.

PASSE, G., *Économies comparés de la France et de la Grande Bretagne*, Paris: Fayard, 1957.

PATTERSON, A. TEMPLE, *The Other Armada. The Franco-Spanish Attempt to Invade Britain in 1779*, Manchester University Press, 1960.

PEARSON, K., *The Life, Letters and Labours of Francis Galton*, Cambridge University Press, 1924.

PEAT, A. N., *Gossip from Paris during the Second Empire*, London: Kegan Paul, Trench & Trubner, 1903.

PERROUX, *The IVth French Plan*, London: National Institute of Econ. and Soc. Research, 1967.

PETERSON, W. C., *The Welfare State in France*, Lincoln: University of Nebraska Press, 1960.

PETRE, F. C., *English Colleges and Convents established on the Continent*, Norwich, 1849.

PICARD, R., *Les Salons Littéraires et la Société Française 1610–1789*, New York: Brentano's, 1943.

PICKLES, D., *The Uneasy Entente*, London: Oxford University Press, 1966.

PIOBETTA, J. B., *Les Institutions universitaires*, Paris, Que-sais je, P.U.F., 487, 1951.

PILLANS, J., 'Seminaries for Teachers', *Edinburgh Review*, lix, 1834, 492–4.

PITTS, J. R., 'Continuity and Change in Bourgeois France' in Stanley Hoffman, Charles P. Kindleberger, Lawrence Wylie, Jesse R. Pitts, Jean-Baptiste Duroselle and Francis Goquel, *France: Change and Tradition*, London: Victor Gollancz, 1963, 271.

Planning (P.E.P.) 'Economic Planning in France', vol. xxvii, No. 454, Aug., 1961.

PRINS, A. A., *French influence in English phrasing*, Leiden: University Press, 1952.

Proceedings of the British Academy 1903–4, London.

'Prophet of European Unity', *Times Literary Supplement*, 16 April, 1938, 257–258.

PURCELL, E. S., *Life of Cardinal Manning, Archbishop of Westminster*, London, 1896, 2 vol.

RAHENBECK, A., 'Les Refugiés belges au 16me siècle en Angleterre', *Revue Trimestrielle*, October 1865.

REES, REV., in *Church Quarterly Review*, January 1908, 307–8, 325–6.

'Returns of aliens dwelling in London', *Huguenot Society Publications*, 1900–1908 .

REYNAUD, *L'Influence Allemande en France au XVIIIe et au XIXe siècle*, Paris: Librairie Hachette, 1922.

'Renaudot's influence in the English Press', *Times Literary Supplement*, 20 January, 1921, 43–44.

RICH, R. W., *The Training of Teachers*, Cambridge University Press, 1933.

RICKARD, P., *Britain in Medieval French Literature 1100–1500*, Cambridge University Press, 1956.

RIDLEY, F., and BLONDEL, J., Public Administration in France, London: Routledge & Kegan Paul, 1964.

RODDIER, HENRI, *J.-J. Rousseau en Angleterre au XVIIIᵉ siècle*, Paris: Boivin, 1948.

ROE, W. G., *Lamennais and England*, London: Oxford University Press, 1966.

ROMER, V. L., 'Matthew Arnold and Some French Poets', *Nineteenth Century*, xciv, 1926.

SACKS, B., *The Religious Issue in the State Schools of England and Wales 1902–1914*, University of New Mexico Press, 1961.

SADLER, SIR M., *Thomas Day. An English Disciple of Rousseau*, Cambridge University Press, 1928.

SARTON, G., *Six Wings: Men of Science in the Renaissance*, London: Bodley Head, 1958.

SAYERS, R. S., 'The Springs of Technical Progress in Britain 1919–1939', *Economic Journal*, lx, 1950, 275–291.

SCHAIBLE, C. H., *The Theory and Practice of Teaching Modern Languages in Schools*, London, 1863.

SCHEIN, J., *Paris Construit*, Paris, 1961.

SCHICKLER, F. DE, *Les Églises du refuge en Angleterre*, Paris, 1892.

SCHOFIELD, R. E., *The Lunar Society of Birmingham*, London: Oxford University Press, 1963.

SCOULOUDI, I., 'Alien Immigration into and Alien Communities in London, 1558–1640', *P.H.S.*, xvi, 1938, 27–49.

SCOULOUDI, I., 'Sir Theodore Turquet de Mayerne. Royal Physician and Writer, 1573–1655', *P.H.S.*, xvi, No. 9, 1940, 301–337.

SCOVILLE, WARREN C., *The Persecution of the Huguenots and French Economic Development 1680–1720*, The University of California Press, 1960.

SEIGNOBOS, *et al*, *La lutte scolaire en France au dix neuvième siècle*, Paris, 1912.

SELLS, I. E., *Matthew Arnold and France: the Poet*, London: Cambridge University Press, 1955.

SENIOR, NASSAU WILLIAM, *Conversations with Distinguished Persons during the Second Empire from 1860–1863*, London: Hurst & Blackett, 1880.

SERJEANTSON, M. S., *A History of Foreign Words in English*, London: Routledge & Kegan Paul, 1961.

SERVAN-SCHREIBER, J-J., *Le Défi Américain*, Paris: Denoël, 1967.

SIEGFRIED, A., *America Comes of Age. A French Analysis*, London: Jonathan Cape, 1927.

SIMON, W. M., *European Positivism in the Nineteenth Century*, Ithaca, Cornell University Press, 1963.

SMART, K. F., 'Vocational Guidance in France and Great Britain', *Technical Education*, 2, No. 3, March, 1960, 11.

SMITH, F., *A History of English Elementary Education*, University of London Press, 1931.

SOUTHERN, R. W., 'England and the Continent in the Twelfth Century', *The Listener*, April 1967, 6, 13, 20.

SPARROW, W. J., *Knight of the White Eagle*, London: Hutchinson's, 1964.

SPRAT, T., *History of the Royal Society*, ed. J. I. Cope and H. W. Jones, St. Louis: Washington University Press, 1958.

STANKIEWILZ, W. J., *Politics and Religion in Seventeenth Century France*, The University of California Press, 1960.

STANLEY, A. P., *The Life and Correspondence of Thomas Arnold, D.D.*, London: Ward, Lock and Co., 1890.

ST. JOHN, B., *Purple Tints of Paris*, London, 1854.

STONE, R., and BROWN, J. A. C., 'A Long-term Growth Model for the British Economy', in R. C. Geary (ed.), *Europe's Future in Figures*, Amsterdam: North Holland Co., 1962.

STOYE, J. W., *English Travellers Abroad 1604–1667*, London: Jonathan Cape, 1952.

SUGGETT, H., 'The Use of French in England in the later Middle Ages', *Transactions of the Royal Historical Society*, 4th Ser., xxviii, 1946, 60–83.

SUPER, R. H., (ed.), *The Complete Prose Works of Matthew Arnold. III. Lectures and Essays in Criticism*, University of Michigan Press, 1962.

SUPER, R. H., (ed.), *The Complete Prose Works of Matthew Arnold. II. Democratic Education*, University of Michigan Press, 1962.

SWART, KOENRAD, W., *The Sense of Decadence in Nineteenth-Century France*, The Hague: Martinus Nijhoff, 1964.

TAPIES, FR. DE LE CHEVALIER, *La France et l'Angleterre du statistique morale et physique de la France comparée à celle d'Angleterre sur toute les points analogues* Versailles: privately printed, 1845.

TAYLOR, S., *On French and German as substitutes for Greek in University Pass examinations*, London, 1870.

TEMPLEMAN, G., 'Edward II and the Beginnings of the Hundred Years War', *Transactions of the Royal Historical Society*, 5th Series, 11, 1952, 66–68.

TEMPLEMAN, W. D., 'Arnold's *Literary Influence of Academies*', *Studies in Philology*, xliii, 1946, 91.

THIBAUDET, ALBERT, *La République des Professeurs*, Paris: Bernard Grasset, 1927.

THOMPSON, D., *Two Frenchmen*, London: Cresset Press, 1954.

THOMSON, DAVID, *The Proposal for Anglo-French Union in 1940*, Oxford: Clarendon Press, 1966.

TOLLN, DR., 'Concerning the name Huguenot', *P.H.S.*, vi, 1901, 327ff.

TOUT, T. F., *France and England: The Relations in the Middle Ages and Now*, Manchester University Press, 1927.

TOOLEY, R. V., 'Map Making in France from the Sixteenth Century to the Eighteenth Century', *P.H.S.*, xviii, No. 6, 1952, 479.

TOPAZIO, V. W., *D'Holbach's Moral Philosophy, its background and development*, Geneva : Institut et Musée Voltaire, 1956.

TORREY, N. L., *Voltaire and the English Deists*, Yale University Press, 1930.

TREVELYAN, G. M., *English Social History*, London : Longmans, Green and Co., 3rd Ed., 1946.

TURNBULL, G. H., *Dury, Hartlib and Comenius*, Liverpool University Press, 1947.

UPHAM, A. H., *French Influence in English Literature from the Accession of Elizabeth to the Restoration*, New York : Columbia University Press, 1908.

VANDAM, A., *An Englishman in Paris*, London, 1865, ii, 166.

VARENBURGH, E., *Histoire des relations diplomatiques entre le comte de Flandre et l'Angleterre au moyen age*, Brussels, 1874.

VOISINE, J. J. J. *Rousseau en Angleterre a l'Époque Romantique*, Paris : Didier, 1956.

WADE, I. O., *The clandestine organization and diffusion of philosophic ideas in France from 1700 to 1750*, Princeton University Press, 1938.

WAGNER, H., 'Pedigrees of Huguenot Families', *P.H.S.*, xiii, No. 2, 1926, 287–300.

WARD, L. F., 'Sociology at the Paris Exposition of 1900', *Report of the Commissioner of Education for the Years 1899–1900*, Washington, 1901, ii, 1451–1593.

WARREN, H. A., 'Technical Education and Vocational Training in France and Great Britain' in *The Crowther Report*, App. III, London : H.M.S.O., 1959.

WATSON, D. R., 'The Politics of Educational Reform in France during the Third Republic 1900–1940'. *Past & Present*. No. 34, 1966, 81–99, and rejoinder by John E. Talbot *Ibid*. No. 36, 1967, 126–130, and reply 131–137.

WATSON, FOSTER, *Beginnings of the Teaching of Modern Subjects in England*, London : Pitman, 1909.

WATSON, FOSTER, 'Notes and Materials on Religious Refugees in Relation to Education in England before the Revocation of the Edict of Nantes 1685', *P.H.S.*, ix, 1909–11, 299–475.

WATSON, R., *Anecdotes of the life of R. W. written by himself at different intervals, and revised in 1814*, London, 1817.

WEILL, G., *Histoire de l'enseignement secondaire en France 1802–1920*, Paris, 1921.

WEINER, M., *The French Exiles 1789–1815*, London: John Murray, 1960.

WEISS, C., *History of the French Protestant Refugees*, London, 1854.

WEISS, S., *Histoire des Refugiés Protestants de France*, Paris, 1853.

WEMYSS REID, REV. T. W., *Memoirs and Correspondence of Lyon Playfair*, London, 1899.

WHARTON, E., *French Ways and their Meaning*, London: Macmillan, 1919.

WHITRIDGE, A., 'Matthew Arnold and Saint-Beuve', *Proceedings of the Modern Language Association*, liii, 1938.

WILSON, R. M., *Early Middle English Literature*, London: Methuen, 1939; French in English England 1100–1300', *History*, xxvi, 1941, 163–73; xxvii, 1943, 37–60.

WICKELGREN, F. L., 'Matthew Arnold's Literary Relations with France', *Modern Language Review*, xxxiii, 1938, 200–214.

WICKWAR, W. H., *Baron d'Holbach*, London: George Allen and Unwin, 1935.

WILLIAMS, G., *Apprenticeship in Europe: The Lesson for Britain*, London: Chapman and Hall, 1963.

WILLIAMS, G. A., 'Hugh Owen, 1804–1881' in *Pioneers of Welsh Education*, Swansea: Faculty of Education, 1964.

WILSON, HAROLD, *Purpose in Politics, Selected Speeches*, London: Weidenfeld and Nicolson, 1964.

WOOLF, VIRGINIA, *The Common Reader*, First Series, 1925, London: Hogarth Press, 1933.

WOLF, A., *A History of Science, Technology and Philosophy in the Eighteenth Century*, London: George Allen and Unwin, 1938.

YATES, F. A., *The French Academies of the Sixteenth Century*, London: The Warburg Institute, 1947.

ZURKO, E. R. DE, *Origins of Functionalist Theory*, New York, 1957.

ZUZA, F., *A. Binet et la pédagogie expérimentale*, Louvain: E. Nauwelaerts, 1948.